An **ICL** Christian Education/Christian School Resource

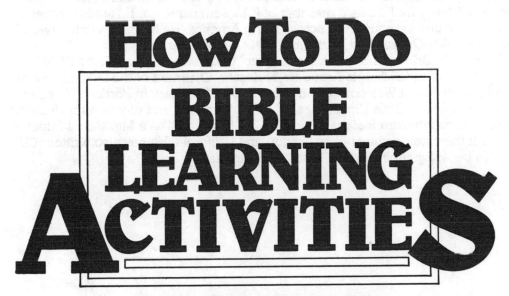

How To Do
BIBLE
LEARNING
ACTIVITIES

GRADES 7-12

by Ed Stewart · Neal McBride
illustrated by Rick Bundschuh

GL International Center for Learning

INTERNATIONAL CENTER FOR LEARNING
A Subsidiary of GL Publications, Ventura, California, U.S.A.

About the Authors

Ed Stewart, the principal author of this book, is Associate Pastor of a church in Oregon. He has a rich background in Christian education, having served as an adult teacher, a youth pastor, an editor of GL's youth and adult curriculum and the youth/adult coordinator for ICL. As a member of ICL's seminar team, Ed leads teacher training seminars in many cities across North America. He has also written two ICL Concept books, *Outreach to Youth* and *How People Learn.*

Dr. Neal McBride, who wrote the chapter "Understanding and Using Bible Learning Activities (BLA's)" is Associate Professor, Chairman of the Department of Church Education at Western Conservative Baptist Seminary in Portland, Oregon. He is a graduate of Biola University and Talbot Seminary and received his doctorate in adult education from Indiana University. He has served as a Minister of Education and a Youth Pastor in churches in Oregon and California. He has also written ICL's Concept book *Equipping Adults Through Bible Study.*

Unless otherwise noted, Scripture quotations are from *The New International Version, Holy Bible.* Copyright © 1978 by New York International Bible Society. Used by permission.

Published by International Center for Learning
GL Publications, Ventura, California 93003.
Printed in U.S.A.

ISBN 0-8307-0851-0

WHERE TO FIND. . .

ART ACTIVITIES

DISCUSSION ACTIVITIES

CREATIVE WRITING

DRAMA ACTIVITIES

MUSIC ACTIVITIES

RESEARCH ACTIVITIES

ORAL PRESENTATION

MISCELLANEOUS ACTIVITIES

PUZZLES AND GAMES

UNDERSTANDING AND USING BIBLE LEARNING ACTIVITIES (BLA's)

This chapter will help you to:
1. Explain what Bible learning activities are and why they are important.
2. Describe the ABC lesson development.
3. Summarize the idea and use of early arrival/fellowship activities.
4. List and gather the basic supplies needed to effectively use BLA's.

GENERAL GUIDELINES

Understanding BLA's

Do the young people in your Sunday School class have the blahs? If you take their blahs and get rid of the "h" (hassle, hodgepodge, hollowness, humdrum, hectic, etc.), what you have left are the BLA's (Bible Learning Activities).

BLA's are the various methods by which a creative teacher involves his or her class members in the first-hand discovery of biblical truth. Let's look a bit closer at the phrase, "Bible learning activity." Moving backwards, the third word ACTIVITY suggests that we want our learners to be active participants in the learning process, not merely passive observers. Meaningless "fun and games," activity for activity's sake, or a group "pooling of ignorance" is not the idea. The object is to select BLA's that directly contribute to the accomplishment of specific learning objectives.

LEARNING indicates that the purpose of the activity is to promote change in the learners. Learning is change; a change in knowledge (facts, information), attitudes (feeling, opinion), and/or behavior (skill, ability). Our task as teachers is to help teenagers change and become more like Jesus Christ. Therefore, a BLA should facilitate learning that leads toward this change process.

Lastly, a BLA is a learning activity that is centered in the BIBLE. God's Word is our standard for both faith and practice. Consequently, a Bible learning activity is a task or method that is centered in helping our students to gain God's perspective as revealed in the Bible.

The Benefit of BLA's

Young people learn best when they are actively involved in the teaching/learning process. According to studies on learning, students who merely "sit and listen" retain significantly less content than those who are personally involved in well-planned learning activities. Students retain 90 percent, after three days, of what they hear, see, and do. Conversely, they retain only 10 percent of what they hear. The point is clear, the more a student is involved the more he/she will learn.

BLA's are merely the methods you provide your class members so that they can "help themselves" to learn spiritual truth. The premise is, don't tell a student something that he can discover for himself. BLA's assist the student to do this very thing. As a result, while simple telling may pass on information, planned involvement leads not only to information but to superior and lasting learning in the largest sense of the idea.

Tips for Guiding Group/Individual Involvement

Proper use of BLA's is very important. Here are some useful tips that have proven to be valuable:

1. How to start Gradually introduce involvement to your class. Begin with low-threat activities. For example:

- Use an involvement activity at the beginning of the hour (the Approach section of the ABC plan outlined on page 8), but use a familiar teaching style for the rest of the hour.
- When people are comfortable with this, use some involvement learning during Conclusion/Decision (at the end of the hour).
- Replace the "opening exercise" with a Fellowship activity.
- Begin using Bible learning activities during Bible Exploration. Start with a low-threat activity such as a neighbor-nudge (two people briefly talk over an assigned topic or question).

2. Clear instructions Whether you are teaching one person or a group of 30 learners, the necessity of clear, simple instructions cannot be overstressed. Verbal instructions should always be accompanied by some type of written instructions. Writing the instructions on the chalkboard, a poster, the overhead, on small index cards, or any other method will help assure that your learners understand what you are asking them to do. Making instructions clear and to the point will make the task easier and more productive for the learners.

3. Leader and recorder When using BLA's that call for small groups (4 to 7 persons), make sure the groups appoint a leader and a recorder. The leader serves to keep the group on track while the recorder takes notes or in some other manner records the group's results. You may need to provide some direction by stating, for example, "The person wearing the most blue will be your leader, and the person who lives the farthest away should be your recorder."

4. Time limits Always state the amount of time the group(s) will have to complete the task. Group members will be more motivated to work if they know there is a time limit. Once or twice during the activity tell them how much time they have left. Learners will often do as much work in the last three minutes of a ten-minute project as they did in the first seven minutes. Remember, time limits are flexible; feel free to add or subtract time as the abilities and interests of your class may necessitate.

5. Encourage students Assure your students that you have confidence in their ability to accomplish the learning activity. By being alert to your students' "comfort level" and selecting activities which you are fairly certain they can handle, your encouragement will be well-founded. Telling them you are available for questions and further explanation will also serve to encourage their efforts.

6. Let them do it! You may know all the answers and may know the best way to complete the task you have assigned, but let your class members find the answers for themselves and do the project with their own minds and hands. Guide them, encourage them, assist them, but let them do it.

7. Needed resources Make certain that you have on hand an ample supply of those materials necessary to complete the activity. Nothing can be more frustrating for your students than not having what they need to finish the task.

8. Reporting results How will you have the individuals or groups report the results of their efforts? Students enjoy hearing or seeing what others have done. In large groups you may ask for a few volunteers to share, or have each group share one idea each before opening it up to further suggestions or comments. Art projects can be affixed to the wall or placed on a bulletin board. Creative songs that apply biblical truth can be sung. The principle is to allow students to benefit from mutual sharing of ideas and results.

9. Be appreciative Thank students for their effort whether they complete their project or not. Every word of appreciation and affirmation is an investment in the future of your class as an involvement-oriented learning experience.

Asking the Right Questions

Fortunately the creative teacher does not have to be skilled in all the arts of group dynamics in order to use BLA's successfully. But learning how to use questions as a teaching tool can be of tremendous value to a teacher. Well-thought-out questions will help learners to identify and evaluate information, to interpret it, and to assess how that information affects their values and decision making. This means you must choose your questions with care. Here are six suggestions that will help you in choosing good questions:

1. Questions should require the learner to think. Avoid asking questions which may be answered with only yes or no.

2. Keep the questions brief and simple, restricting each question to only one main thought. Often we confuse our students by actually asking several questions within one question. Make certain your questions are clearly focused.

3. Distinguish between a question asking for facts and one seeking feelings or opinions.

4. Avoid asking questions which the group cannot answer because of a lack of information or background. Also, stay away from highly personal questions as discussion starters. Many a group discussion has failed to get off the ground because a well-meaning teacher began with a question that learners were afraid to answer.

5. The questions should be a natural part of the class session, not something artificially tacked on at the end to fill some time.

6. The tone and manner of your questions should encourage the learners to express themselves. A friendly, pleasant and sincere tone of voice will encourage confidence and understanding. Remember, while every contribution may not be worthwhile, every *contributor* is!

Keeping in mind these basic suggestions for good questioning, let's examine three different types of questions that you can use:

Informational Questions An informational question requires the learner to remember or refer to specific facts in order to answer the question correctly. A teacher can discern how well a learner knows the basic facts or guide the discovery of those facts by the proper use of an informational question.

Examples: Where was Jesus born? According to Matthew 20:21, what was Jesus' answer to the rich young man? What was the name of the river in which Jesus was baptized?

It is almost impossible to have a meaningful discussion guided by informational questions alone. Therefore, we also need analytical questions.

Analytical Questions Analytical questions encourage learners to attach meaning or explore principles in facts. Questions of this type are more open-ended than informational questions. By using this type of question the teacher helps learners share what they understand and perceive about the facts.

Examples: What do you think Jesus had in mind when He said . . .? How do you think Jesus felt when He was being questioned by Pilate? What are some possible reasons that caused Peter to deny Jesus three times?

Personal Questions Personal questions seek to draw personal application of facts, draw out a learner's values, and explore attitudes. Questions on this level are effective means for engaging learners in the process of reflecting, expressing and acting on concerns that relate to them personally. The focus of these questions is to guide learners in their own decision making and value forming.

Examples: If you had been an apostle what would you have done when Jesus was arrested? How does your life reflect the model we have in Jesus Christ? What is your idea of being "Christ-like"?

ABC LESSON DEVELOPMENT

Bible learning activities are appropriate for all three sections of the ABC lesson format. To illustrate, three examples are presented below for each of the three session parts—Approach to the Word, Bible Exploration, and Conclusion and Decision.

Approach to the Word

Each session should begin with a learning activity designed to capture the interest of your class and introduce the theme of the session. The idea is to whet their appetites for the Bible study that follows. Here are three Approach ideas that could be used with a lesson on the Old Testament figure Elijah taken from I Kings 19:

1. Tape a length of butcher paper to the chalkboard and divide it into three sections. Divide the class into three groups and have group one define fear and write their definition in section one. Have the second group list things that make today's Christians afraid. In the third section have the third group list things people do when they are afraid.

2. Present the following situation to students: You are rappelling. You make a wrong move and find yourself dangling by a rope off the edge of a cliff. From somewhere you hear a voice cry, "If you let go I'll catch you!" but you cannot see who said it or where the person is. Now ask students what they would feel in this situation and what they would be thinking. What would help them trust the voice? What would make that difficult?

3. Ask each student to think of one time he/she was really afraid. Have students tell a neighbor how they felt and what they did in that circumstance.

Bible Exploration

The Bible Exploration is the heart of your class session because it involves each learner directly in the study of God's Word. It is during this portion of the session that you have your learners, through the Exploration activity that you choose to use, explore and discover what the Bible says and means, and discuss its implications for life today. A wide variety of methods is possible. Using the same passage we used in the previous section on the Approach to the Word, here are three possible Bible Exploration activities:

1. Have groups read the passage and make a collage depicting the events in the life of Elijah as found in that chapter.

2. Using a tape recorder, have the students play the characters involved and record a radio interview that focuses on the events, attitudes, and feelings potentially experienced by the characters.

3. Prepare a series of 5 to 10 questions that can facilitate a discussion on the passage. Guide students to talk about their feelings and fears that may be similar to those experienced by Elijah.

Conclusion and Decision

After having spent the majority of the class time discussing what God's Word says and means, each learner needs to apply the truths of Scripture to his or her own life. Questions such as, "What is Scripture asking of me?" or "How can I put it into practice in my own life?" are the main thrust of this section of the lesson plan. The Conclusion and Decision activity may be so personal in nature that you will not want to ask your students to share with each other. Other times, however, it will be very appropriate to gather in small groups and report how the Scriptures previously studied apply to their personal relationships to God and others. Here are three possible Conclusion and Decision activities:

1. Have students select a prayer partner and pray for each other in light of the biblical truth studied.

2. Write the following statement on the board, "Lord, it seems to me you do expect too much of me sometimes, but I'm willing to try again in regards to . . ." Have each student complete the sentence by writing his/her answer on a piece of paper. Close the session with a time of silent prayer giving students the opportunity to bring their response before God.

3. Ask students to suggest ways that they, with God's help, can help one another handle fear and discouragement. List suggestions on the board (or overhead) as they are given. Ask each student to select one thing to do next week in this area for someone else. Close in prayer, asking for the strength and willingness to do that one thing.

Choosing/Evaluating the Best Method

What method is best for each part of the ABC lesson plan? The answer to this question is hard because most BLA's can be used in a variety of ways for each part of the lesson. For example, consider how "writing a prayer" could be used:

For the Approach: The leader begins by telling a story. "A Christian teenager has been ordered by his school principal to stop sharing his faith on campus. After leaving the principal's office, the student stops to pray." Write what you think you would pray in that situation. Allow time for writing, then guide the learners into the lesson.

For the Bible Exploration: After reading Acts 3:1-11, write a prayer the healed man might have prayed after entering the Temple. Write a prayer of thanks from a person who has just received Christ as Saviour.

For the Conclusion and Decision: Write a short prayer to God, asking for specific help with a specific problem that you are willing to commit to Him this week.

When selecting any method, remember that your choice should be based on:
1. the object or purpose of the session;
2. the length of time available;
3. the needs and interests of your class members;
4. an understanding of how people learn;

5. the equipment and facilities available;

6. your own ability to use a particular method.

Remember, in selecting a BLA, variety and selectivity are keys. Stay away from using the same methods week after week. We all know that variety is the spice of life. This is also a big key in maintaining the interest of your students. Also, select BLA's that are appropriate for the content they are to be used with. Ask yourself the question, "Will this method accurately communicate the truth I want my students to gain?" If yes, use it; if not, select another.

Here is a list of additional criteria by which you can evaluate the Bible learning activities you are considering for any session. If the methods you select do not seem appropriate, adapt them or change them until they meet the learning objectives you have outlined.

1. The method should help direct attention to the specific nature of the learning task so that the learner will know what is expected. Is the learner expected to discuss, ask questions, give opinions or write? Clearly state what you expect each person to do.

2. A method should arouse interest and motivate the individual to want to learn about the subject being presented. Does the method put class members to sleep or make them sit up and say, "I want to know more about what you just said."?

3. A method should also be able to maintain interest. When more of the senses (hearing, seeing, etc.) are involved, interest will be greater.

4. A good teaching method avoids causing excessive frustration or failure on the part of the learner. Any method that continuously frustrates or does not allow success is not effective. Do your learners understand the terms you use? Are your visuals clear and accurate? Are your instructions clear? Are you asking people to do something they will feel comfortable about?

5. A teaching method should help the person transfer what has been learned to everyday life outside of class.

6. A method should help develop and maintain positive attitudes toward the teacher, the subject being taught and toward the learner himself/herself.

7. A method should fit the time limits in which it must fit and be appropriate to the section purpose of the ABC lesson plan.

EARLY ARRIVALS/FELLOWSHIP

The Bible learning activities spoken of thus far and presented in this book are mainly designed to be used within the ABC lesson format, or, in general, within your class period. So, what are you to do with early arrivals? One suitable answer to this question is to plan an informal activity that students can become involved in until it is time for class to begin. But more than just a time filler, this "early arrival activity" can be an effective tool in building an atmosphere of warmth and acceptance among your students that is so vital to group learning experiences. It is an opportunity to help your students get to know and appreciate each other and to establish lines of communication.

This is also a good time to make a point of greeting visitors. Prior to the activity, select two or three individuals who are responsible to greet newcomers and make them feel welcome. It is a good idea to have name tags available each week for all your class members. When everyone is wearing a name tag, visitors feel more comfortable and even "old timers" will appreciate the help name tags provide.

The following activities are a few examples of early arrival activities that are designed to encourage nonthreatening openness among class members. Select or adapt one of these activities to precede each of your class sessions. Provide some type of refreshment if it is appropriate for your class, but be sure to have an activity prepared to stimulate meaningful sharing. Not only will this actively involve your early arrivers, but it will likely make your other class members want to arrive on time.

The Title Is Me: Write on the chalkboard, flipchart or overhead transparency approximately 10 best-selling book titles or current film titles. Have each person study the list and select a title which says something about the past week he has experienced. Ask volunteers to share their title and a sentence of explanation with the class.

Meaningful Scriptures: Have volunteers share with the class a verse from the Bible which has been particularly meaningful to them within the last month. Be sure to have each person explain why the verses were meaningful.

Why Come? Have class members circulate in the group, answering the question, "Why do you attend this Bible class?"

Ideal Vacation: Give each person a sheet of paper on which to draw some symbol that represents his or her ideal vacation. Have people share these in groups of four, or display them on the bulletin board for all to see.

Task-Oriented Name Tags: Provide colored paper, scissors, felt pens and pins. Ask each person to select a color of paper and cut it into a shape which represents a major task in life (for a fireman, a fire hat; for a homemaker, a rolling pin; etc.). Then have each person write his or her name on the cutout and pin it to his clothing. Allow time for people to discuss briefly their task with others at random.

I'm Lonely: Have students gather in clusters of three or four and share one experience when they were lonely and how they handled it.

Personal Coat of Arms: See page 28. Allow about five minutes for drawing. Then have people share these with each other in groups of three.

Life Goals: Have class members gather in small groups and share one life goal with each other. If time permits, have them talk about how they hope to accomplish that goal.

Personal Church History: Give each person a sheet of paper on which to complete this brief questionnaire.

1. When did you first attend this church (or group)?
2. What person(s) was most responsible for your attendance?
3. What was your first impression of the people?

Have people gather in clusters of three or four and share answers with one another.

Instant Inheritance: Have class members jot down their answers to the following question on a small index card and share it with others in groups of three: "If I could wish my children anything at all for an inheritance, what three things would I wish for them?"

I'm Thankful: Write the following incomplete statement on the chalkboard, flipchart or overhead transparency: "Today I'm thankful for . . ." Ask class members to think for one minute about how they would finish that statement. Then have people gather in clusters of three or four and share their answers.

Name, Rank and Cereal Number: As class members arrive ask them to form pairs and share their full name, the state or country of birth, and their favorite food.

Home Sweet Home: Have students share with two other individuals what city they consider to be their "hometown" and how long it has been since they last visited it.

R and R: Write the following statement on the chalkboard or overhead transparency: "Where is your favorite vacation spot and when were you there last?" Ask adults to form groups of three and share their answers with each other.

A Few of My Favorite Things: Distribute plain sheets of paper to students as they arrive. Instruct students to number from one to five and make a list of the things in life that they love to do. Have them specify which things they would not have listed five years ago. Encourage students to compare lists with at least one other person during the fellowship time.

Fantasy Island: As students enter the classroom, have them respond in pairs or triads to this statement, "If money were no object, I would like to visit (name of country) for one month. The first thing I would do is _____." Have statement written on chalkboard or overhead.

So Far So Good: Have class members share with one another the most meaningful thing they have learned so far in their study of the course. After five minutes, ask for several volunteers to share their responses.

In Living Color: Ask students to form groups of three and share their favorite colors and why they like those colors. Then ask them to recall what colors are mentioned in the Bible.

May Flowers? Distribute plain sheets of colored paper and ask students to tear a shape that represents what they like about the current month. Have each student share their paper tear with at least two other people.

A Little Dab'll Do Ya: Before class members arrive, write the following instructions: "Form pairs and discuss and defend your way of applying toothpaste to your toothbrush. Now find one person who shares your method and one who does not."

Tennis Anyone? As students arrive, have them neighbor-nudge about the last competitive sports event in which they participated or paid to see; which sports they enjoy; and/or which sports they least enjoy.

Birthday Buddies: As students arrive, ask them to find the person in the class who has the birthday closest to theirs. Then have them share with each other their most special birthday.

They're Playing My Song: Ask class members to think of a song whose title or lyrics capture the quality of their recent week, or deal with something they have been thinking about all week. Ask people to share their song titles or lyrics with at least one other person during the fellowship time.

MATERIALS AND EQUIPMENT

To use BLA's effectively, you will need to collect and have on hand a number of different materials and equipment. Here is a checklist to help you. For every item you cannot check off, make creative plans for improvement.

Your classroom should possess the following characteristics to be appropriate for learning activities:
- ☐ 10 square feet minimum for each student
- ☐ Adequate lighting
- ☐ Proper ventilation

- ☐ Heating and cooling systems are functioning
- ☐ Acoustics are good
- ☐ Can be darkened enough for films or slides
- ☐ Electrical outlets are accessible
- ☐ Comfortable chairs, preferably ones which can be moved
- ☐ Tables to work at (or just sit around)
- ☐ Chalkboard, chalk, and eraser
- ☐ At least one bulletin board
- ☐ A screen or light-colored blank wall for projection

A supply of these items should be in the classroom at all times:
- ☐ Chalk
- ☐ Pencils or pens
- ☐ Felt marking pens
- ☐ Writing paper
- ☐ Drawing paper
- ☐ Masking tape
- ☐ Scissors
- ☐ Glue
- ☐ Newsprint tablet or roll of shelf or butcher paper
- ☐ Some discarded pictorial magazines
- ☐ Index cards
- ☐ A ball of string
- ☐ Paper clips

The following resource items should be available in the classroom for in-class use and check out:
- ☐ Extra Bibles, various versions
- ☐ Concordances
- ☐ Bible dictionary
- ☐ English dictionary
- ☐ Bible atlas
- ☐ Bible handbook
- ☐ Assorted Bible commentaries
- ☐ Christian books and periodicals

The following equipment may be available (shared with other classes) for optional use:
- ☐ Overhead projector
- ☐ Slide projector
- ☐ Filmstrip projector
- ☐ Motion picture projector
- ☐ Tape recorder
- ☐ Video tape recorder
- ☐ Personal computer
- ☐ Record player

Gathering Materials

As for gathering materials, here's a helpful tip: Leaf through your teacher's manual and make a shopping list from the "Materials Needed" section and the "Session Preparation" list that is usually included with each session plan. Take a couple of hours to gather the supplies you will need for the next few weeks or an entire quarter and store them in the classroom or at home for ready use. Check with your superintendent—perhaps your expenses may be reimbursed through the Sunday School or Christian education budget.

SELECTION CODES

You are now ready to begin using the various BLA suggestions presented in this book. To help you in your selection, a coding system has been used after the name of each activity. Each BLA is coded in two ways to help a teacher in selecting an activity.

1. The shaded part(s) of the arrow = the section(s) of a lesson which are most appropriate for that BLA. (A = Approach to the Word; B = Bible Exploration; C = Conclusion and Decision.)

2. The placement of the arrow designates the age-level for which the BLA is most appropriate. For example, an arrow above the left half of the age-level bar designates an activity that is most appropriate for junior high students. An arrow at the middle of the bar designates an activity that is appropriate for both junior and senior high. An arrow above the right half of the bar designates an activity that is best for senior high students.

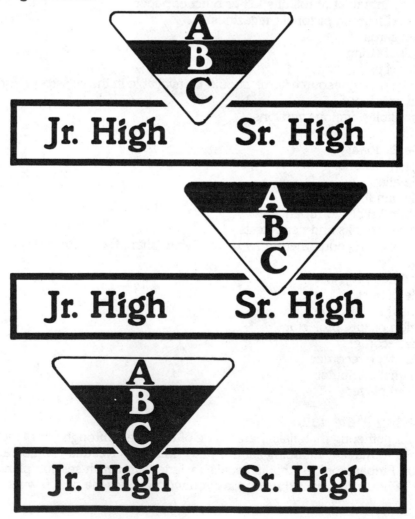

THE SIGHTS AND SOUNDS OF BIBLE LEARNING

Audio/Visual Aids Which Can Help Your Lessons Live!

Audio/visual aids are vehicles which help the teacher convey the intangible truth of God to the immaterial hearts of the learners through the gateway of the physical senses (seeing, hearing, feeling, tasting, smelling). What we see, hear and touch during a Bible study session can make a difference in how effectively God's Word enters our hearts. The more we see, hear and touch—and the more we do these simultaneously—the more we learn. Though not as widely employed as the first three, the senses of taste and smell can also contribute to a positive learning experience (a fresh-smelling, fragrant classroom and occasional refreshments for the learners).

Many audio/visual tools have been present in the church for decades. But recent technological advances have opened up a new gold mine of audio/visual opportunity for the resourceful Bible teacher. Some of the tools we have in our hands today did not even exist in the imagination two generations ago. And other aids and equipment, which were desirable but financially impractical for the church, have been perfected and simplified, and are now within the economic reach of even the smaller church or school.

The message we teach and the persons we are teaching are the most important elements in the Bible teaching ministry. Yet the media we choose to communicate the message to those we teach can either expedite or hinder the process. In Bible teaching, the medium is *not* the message. But the medium can greatly assist or hinder the message. With our focus solidly on the message—God's written and living Word—and on the learners—young men and women God brings into our classroom—we are free to investigate and utilize any and all available means which will assist in uniting the two.

The audio/visual catalog which follows will do three things: (1) remind you of some time-honored tools which are still useful today; (2) update you on some solidly contemporary equipment and supplies; and (3) introduce you to some fairly recent newcomers in the sight, sound and feel of learning.

REMEMBER: What is true of teaching *methods* is also true of teaching *tools* — variety is the key. The same methods and tools used every week will detract from the effectiveness of the teaching experience. But using a variety of methods and tools will keep learners interested and open.

Oldies but Goodies

1. **Chalkboard** The classroom chalkboard remains a most economical and accessible medium for providing eye involvement for learners. It's economical because, once a chalkboard is purchased, it can render years of service without needing replacement. Purchasing a box of chalk every few months and replacing a lost eraser from time to time require minimal cash outlay. The chalkboard is accessible because wall-mounted and portable chalkboards have been standard teaching equipment for years. Most churches and schools already have a number of them.

The chalkboard can be used by teacher and learners alike for listing, outlining, illustrating and diagramming lesson material. Colored chalk can add variety and interest. Information on the chalkboard, written before the class session begins, can be hidden from view by paper taped to the board and revealed at the appropriate time.

A classroom chalkboard, frequently cleaned, well-stocked with fresh chalk and creatively used, can be a primary eye-involvement tool.

2. Filmstrip projector If you are not using the filmstrip projector today because you remember these projectors to be cumbersome, noisy, difficult to load and operate, and expensive, you have a pleasant surprise coming. Filmstrip projectors are available today which are compact, quiet, easy to use and quite affordable. And there are some new materials available which make the filmstrip projector more usable than ever.

Commercially-produced filmstrips often come with soundtracks on records, but many are now available with convenient audio cassette sound tracks (cassette players are generally more portable than record players). Sound tracks from records can also be transferred to cassette tape.

Learners can make their own non-photographic filmstrips using clear filmstrip celluloid which can be purchased at many photo supply stores. Using special transparency pens, learners write or draw on the clear celluloid strip—highlighting a Bible narrative with simple pictures, listing and/or illustrating the main points in the lesson or illustrating the lyrics to a song. The celluloid can then be fed into the filmstrip projector to display the learners' work on the screen. Accompanying music or narration—live or on cassette tape—enhances the presentation.

3. Maps Unless you can afford to transport your learners to Bible lands to acquaint them with cities, countries, mountains and rivers mentioned in the Bible, you need a good supply of classroom maps. In addition to maps identifying geographic information in biblical times, each classroom needs contemporary maps showing countries which occupy biblical locations today.

Good, commercial wall maps are available in a variety of sizes, qualities and costs. Transparency maps for overhead projectors can also be purchased. A more economical approach to classroom maps—one which could include learners—is a map-making project. Learner-made maps can be as colorful and detailed as the class members like. They can also be three-dimensional—using inverted paper cups for mountains, blue cellophane strips for rivers, "Monopoly" hotels and houses for cities, etc. Learners can also make colorful and creative overhead transparency maps, using blank transparencies and transparency pens.

4. Picture file Someone once said, "A picture is worth a thousand words." The saying is especially true for the Bible teaching classroom—pictures can effectively reinforce lesson topics and principles. One way to accommodate this fact is a picture file—a collection of pictures clipped from magazines, newspapers, posters or any other source available.

A picture of skid-row derelicts to illustrate lack of direction, a war scene to portray hatred in the unregenerate heart, a child helping a friend illustration portraying the childlike love we are to have toward one another—all are pictures which can be readily found in various publications.

A teacher can train himself/herself to be alert to pictures which may be useful in the future. A picture file, organized by theme, can keep pictures ready for the right moment.

5. Record player Though many of its functions are often more easily accomplished on an audio cassette player, the record player can still assist in classroom teaching and learning. Even a modest stereo system can provide "atmosphere" for learning by playing music before, during or after the class session. Playing recorded music in order to compare lyrics with Bible principles can be done on a record player. Furthermore, recorded speeches, dramatizations and interviews can assist in driving home the point of a lesson.

Solid Contemporaries

1. Audio cassette player With the advent of efficient and economical electronics, it is possible for many churches to place an inexpensive cassette player in every classroom. A wide variety of teaching avenues is opened when a cassette player is present: a growing library of cassette tapes on Bible topics; several Scripture-on-cassette versions to use in class occasionally for Scripture reading; music for enjoyment and lyric study.

If the cassette *player* is also a *recorder*, many more options are present: in-class "radio" programs produced by learners; imaginary interviews of Bible characters and real interviews of other learners or adult church members on various topics of study. A class can use the recorder/player as a ministry tool to send a tape to a class member who has been hospitalized or has moved away, or to a missionary. Battery-operated cassette player/recorders have even greater utility for movement around the classroom, church or community.

2. Flipchart A flipchart can be as simple as a large pad of paper tacked to a bulletin board or as elaborate as a commercially-produced, wall-mounted cabinet concealing a retractable aluminum easel and paper.

The essentials are the paper and a way to display it.

A flipchart can be used, like a chalkboard, for spontaneous listing, illustrating and diagramming—with a fresh sheet of paper ready under each sheet the teacher uses. Felt markers are an inexpensive and colorful writing instrument for the flipchart—water-based markers minimize the danger of permanent staining of clothing or walls or furniture.

A carefully prepared flipchart can be an attention-keeping device during a time of teacher lecture—with each turn of the chart a new picture, diagram or illustration appears, which reinforces the teacher's message. Learners can also prepare their own flipchart presentations as part of their Scripture study. Newsprint paper is the most economical flipchart resource. It can be purchased in pads or in non-padded bulk to be stapled, taped or tacked to a useable display surface.

3. Opaque projector Though not as accessible as other media, the opaque projector offers some unique possibilities when it can be rented, borrowed or purchased. The opaque projector magnifies and projects the image of items onto a screen. It helps an entire classroom of learners see something which ordinarily would need to be passed from hand to hand to be seen. Therefore a teacher could project pages from an open book, a small map, drawing or diagram, and even a small object (signet ring, coin, etc.) for all to see. The opaque projector can be used by teachers in illustrating lecture and by learners in sharing items with the class.

Public schools which own opaque projectors can sometimes be persuaded to loan or rent their equipment for weekend use. Such an arrangement may be economically more desirable than purchasing an opaque projector.

4. Overhead projector Like the cassette player, the overhead projector is much more economically accessible to churches than when first introduced. The overhead projector uses a shadow principle to cast an enlarged image on the screen from a clear transparency marked with special transparency pens. Greater utility has been added to the overhead projector with the introduction of colored transparencies, colored pens, continuous rolls of celluloid which can be mounted on some projectors, transparency-making kits (colored transparencies, transfer letters, numbers, diagrams, symbols, etc.), overlays and professionally-produced maps, diagrams and outlines. Many photocopy machines have the capacity to produce transparencies from dark-on-light originals, making the possibilities for classroom use almost endless.

Instead of listing their discoveries on the chalkboard, learners can take blank transparencies and transparency pens and list, illustrate or diagram their assignment for projection on the classroom screen.

5. Slide projector The slide projector can be used—with professionally-produced or homemade photographic slides—to visualize for the classroom any number of items—Bible lands, current events, pictures of Bible principles being acted out, etc. Such presentations can be prepared by the teachers and/or learners outside of class for classroom presentation, or by the learners during class (arranging slides into an order corresponding to a script or outline).

Variety can be added to slide presentations by involving learners in producing non-photographic slides. Mounted blank slides, which can be written or drawn on using transparency pens, can be purchased at photo and/or school supply stores. In addition, clear adhesive material can be cut into the size of slides, peeled to expose the sticky surface and adhered to a glossy surface such as clay-base magazine paper. When the paper and clear film are firmly adhered, the slide may be placed in water to soak. After brief soaking, the paper may be rubbed off leaving the ink on the slide. The slide may then be mounted and projected, producing an interesting effect.

Learners may be given passages of Scripture or lyrics to hymns or songs to illustrate with photographic and/or non-photographic slides.

6. Listening/viewing centers Another classroom use of various cassette players and filmstrip and/or slide projectors is the listening/viewing center. Areas in the classroom can be designated as a listening center or viewing center by providing the appropriate equipment for learners to experience individually or in small groups cassette tapes, slides, filmstrips on the basis of personal interest. If the room is large enough, two or more centers may be established far enough apart from each other so as not to be disruptive. Reasonably-priced sets of headphones can be purchased and multiple jacks supplied for cassette players so that a small group of learners can listen to a cassette tape privately without disturbing the rest of the class.

Recent Newcomers

1. Marker board On the same principle as the chalkboard, the commercially-produced marker board is a smooth-surfaced, framed board which is designed to be written on with a specially prepared felt tip marker. The marker board outshines the chalkboard in that the contrast is much brighter and the colors of the markers are much more brilliant than the effect of colored chalk on the chalkboard. The marker board may be erased (providing the correct markers are used on it) with no residue of chalkdust.

2. Movies/projector As with other technological advances, the 8mm camera,

18

projector and film have come within economic reach of the Bible study classroom. If such equipment is not owned by the church or school or their constituents, it may be rented at nominal costs. Filmmaking has many of the same qualities as slidemaking, mentioned earlier, but with the added dimension of continuous action. Films may be made outside of class which will portray a Bible narrative, illustrate a principle in action or provide an open-ended drama for in-class response. As much or more actual learning may take place outside the classroom with the crew making the film as in the classroom viewing and responding to the film. A film may be a unit or quarter project, with some editing or scripting taking place in the classroom.

3. **Instant print cameras** Another piece of accessible photographic equipment is the instant print camera, now available in several economical models. The instant print camera can be used alone or in conjunction with a cassette player to illustrate lesson themes. Instant photos can be taken as part of an in-class or outside-of-class Bible study project as learners discuss and dramatize Bible narratives or principles. Pictures can be mounted in story strips for classroom display or in photo albums to read as books. Instant print photos are also useful to keep a record of, or display of, class members and/or class activities on a bulletin board.

4. **Video cassette player** Though not yet in the economic bracket of most other audio/visual tools, the video cassette player is a rising star to be considered in the Bible study classroom. Again, refinements in technology and mass production are forcing the initial costs of the video player down and many education institutions consider video taping no longer to be a luxury but a necessity. With the availability of the players comes also the availability of the cameras for classroom use, combining the values of 8mm filming with instant print photography. In-class dramatizations of Scripture, simulated TV interviews, game show format Bible quizzes and other possibilities are open when video equipment is available.

In addition, professionally-produced video cassette tapes are becoming available on countless Bible study themes. Such tapes can be used to augment in-class Bible study involvement and, in some cases, at-home learner reference.

HELP THEM SEE
WHAT YOU'RE SAYING

How to Involve Learners During Oral Presentations

Studies in learning have revealed that we retain only about 10-15 percent of what we hear. Yet much of the activity in the Bible study classroom is centered on speaking and listening—teacher to learner, learner to teacher, learner to learner. Furthermore, the venerable granddaddy of all teaching methods is the lecture— learners listen while teacher talks.

The lecture method and other methods of oral presentation in the classroom are not bad teaching methods. Often, lecture is the most efficient way of presenting a block of material in a limited amount of time, although the statistics of retention indicate that the learners come away from the lecture with significantly less than if they were more actively involved with the content.

In order to capitalize on the efficiency of the oral presentation methods without sacrificing the increased retention of more active learning methods, take advantage of a variety of oral presentation aids designed to maximize the lecture and other "up-front" presentations.

The following five categories of oral presentation aids will give the lecture-prone teacher plenty of ideas for bringing greater levels of learner involvement to oral presentation methods:

1. Audio/visuals When the teacher adds to his verbal presentation something specific for his learners to look at, the percentages of retention jump from 10-15 percent to about 50 percent. So it is most important that some kind of visual activity accompany the audio activity of listening: Listing main points on the chalkboard, flipchart or overhead transparency as they are being spoken; illustrating factual information by using large and attractive maps, graphs, charts, diagrams or pictures; visualizing lecture content with slides, films, video cassettes or objects relating to the theme. Anything that will underscore visually what the teacher is presenting orally will assist the learner in retaining a greater amount of the content.

A more thorough description of audio/visual aids available for the Bible teaching classroom will be found in the article "The Sights and Sounds of Bible Learning" on page 15 of this manual.

2. Demonstration Another way to visualize an oral presentation is to demonstrate the information or principles being verbalized. When lecturing on the contents of the Tabernacle, a teacher might prepare a model of the Tabernacle and place each piece of furniture in the model as he/she describes it. When discussing the Last Supper, the teacher may set a table in the classroom as it might have been set for the feast and indicate the location and significance of the bread and wine. The concepts of Romans 6 might be demonstrated with paper chains attached from the teacher to a person or poster representing the sin nature and another person or poster representing new life in Christ.

The demonstration adds some action to the visual element and thus increases interest and involvement.

3. Forum A forum is an open group discussion which follows an oral presentation such as a monologue, panel, Bible reading or recitation, debate or interview. Learners are encouraged to record their ideas and questions during the oral presentation and to voice these at its conclusion. A forum may be presented in a formal style with each learner giving a prepared response in turn, or in an informal style with learners dialoging with the presenters in conversational style.

Learners who are actively involved in saying and doing something in the learning process are said to retain upwards to 90 percent of the activity. Thus the activity of writing comments and questions during an oral presentation, and then talking through them during a forum period, enhances the oral presentation.

4. Question/answer As with the forum method, the question/answer method of involvement moves learners to do and say something in response to oral presentations. Several varieties of question/answer are possible: (1) Learners write questions to ask the presenter(s) at the conclusion of the presentation; (2) the presenter(s) give learners a list of questions which will be answered during the presentation, so learners listen and write answers; (3) presenter(s) may ask questions of the learners at the conclusion of the presentation to review the content; (4) presenter(s) may give learners a written quiz at the conclusion of the presentation.

5. Worksheet Another way to involve learners actively in oral presentation content is to place in their hands a worksheet and a pen or pencil with instructions as to what should be written or drawn during the presentation. The worksheet may be as simple as a blank sheet of paper for general note-taking, or as complex as a detailed outline or diagram for learners to follow and/or write on. Ample space should be provided on the worksheet for learners to write responses, answer questions, complete diagrams, etc.

Once again, the activity of writing while listening deepens the learning experience and encourages retention. The attractiveness of the worksheet can be a factor in the learners' desire to be involved. Adding artwork and using bright colored paper can invite their involvement.

It is often helpful for the worksheet to be reproduced or simulated in larger form for display in the classroom. An overhead transparency, poster or outline on the chalkboard to which the teacher refers will help the learners follow the same topics on their worksheets.

TIPS FOR GROUPING LEARNERS

Bible learning activities can be used in teaching groups as small as two and as large as can be crowded into a classroom. And within a given class period, the teacher may utilize several different groupings of learners to facilitate the lesson aims and strategies. For example, a department of 20 learners may begin a lesson in a large group completing a graffiti poster on the wall during a five-minute Approach activity. Then learners may gather for 20 minutes in three groups of six to explore and discuss Bible verses on the lesson theme. The three groups open into one large circle as each group reports their discoveries to the large group for 10 minutes. Then learners may talk in pairs for five minutes listing ways their Scripture passage might apply to teens today, and each pair returns to its group of six to share its list. Finally, individual volunteers may speak to the large group, stating their personal response to the Bible study.

Every different grouping has its value to the learning process. Large groups are most helpful during times of leader input or information sharing which is pertinent to the entire class. Small groups encourage learner interaction and involvement which is so vital to the success of an individual's learning experience. But how does a teacher know when to employ the different groupings? How can a class move from large group to pairs to small groups to large group most efficiently and with the least amount of classroom disruption?

The following tips will serve as some general guidelines for utilizing various kinds of groupings in the youth classroom:

1. Know Your Activities and Class Members

Some learning activities require a certain sized group. A group discussion works best with a group of five to eight learners and is not as productive with a group of 20 because some members will not be able to participate in a group that large. Study the requirements of each learning activity to discover the right sized group to accomplish it. Also, be aware that some class members function best in certain sized groups. Utilize a variety of groupings which will catch the interest of the maximum number of learners.

2. Know Your Schedule and Facilities

The time schedule of a class session will suggest which groupings are appropriate for the lesson. If 10 minutes are allowed for discovering several principles from a chapter of Scripture, a teacher's illustrated summary with a large group would serve the need better than smaller groups reading, discussing, listing and reporting to the large group, which would take much longer. Classroom size, seating arrangement and facilities will also serve as clues to which groupings will be the most productive. A classroom with moveable, individual chairs will serve a number of grouping arrangements whereas fixed seating (pews, chairs bolted together, etc.) will limit grouping possibilities.

3. Avoid "Dividing" and "Separating"

When giving instructions for grouping, avoid negative and possibly threatening terms like "dividing the class" or "separating into groups." Such terms may cause learners to feel that they are being alienated from each other. Rather, suggest that learners "move" into groups of three, "gather" four chairs together, "rearrange" the circle into clusters of six or "form" pairs.

4. Give Specific Guidelines for Groupings

It is more time efficient and helpful to learners for the teacher to state specific size and location of the groups desired. Rather than saying, "Let's get into several small groups," state exactly how many groups, how many in each group and where the groups should form. "We are going to move into three groups with no more than five and no fewer than four learners in each group. One group will form by the door, one by the table and one next to the window." Often the teacher will want to preassign learners to groups based on their level of participation: "Group one will consist of Marci, Kris, Charisse and Lynette. Will you four girls move your chairs into a circle next to the table?"

5. Give Choices Where Appropriate

The teacher should decide which groupings will best suit the lesson aims, but often learners should be allowed to choose which group they will join. "We are now gathering into three work groups with no more than six in a group. You may choose which work group you would like to join—Group 1 will be working on an interview, Group 2 will do a mural and Group 3 will prepare a pantomime."

6. Give Signals for Groupings

It is often helpful to say, "When I say 'go,' move your chairs into circles of five . . . Go!" Such signals (you can create your own verbal or non-verbal 'go') will minimize movement in the classroom while valuable instructions are being given as to what learners will be doing in their new groups. Also, giving time signals during activities will help coordinate movement in class: "In two minutes we will return to our large circle . . . One minute to complete our group work . . . Now would you please open up your small circles and let's form one large circle."

7. Let the Seating Say It

Before the class session begins, arrange the chairs into the groupings which will suit the first learning activity—large circle, three rows facing front, circles of six chairs, etc. Such preparation will minimize possible confusion at the beginning of the class session as to where learners should begin. NOTE: "Circles" of chairs (5-8) often are more functional when arranged in "horseshoe" shape with the open end toward the front of the room. Such an arrangement will allow all the learners a better view of the chalkboard, screen, flipchart and leader during class work.

8. Seek Adult Leadership

Most groups of teen learners will be more productive when an adult leader is present in the group to provide guidance and assistance. The adult leader should not do all the work or give all the answers in the group, but should function as a co-learner and guide to help the group complete its task. In some situations, learners may work in pairs or trios for short periods without direct adult leadership.

9. Suggest a Starting Point

Sometimes a small study or sharing group will waste valuable time trying to decide who should speak first. The teacher can eliminate this lapse by stating in his/her instructions, ". . . and begin with the person in your group who is wearing the most blue" or "the person whose birthday is closest to today" or some other appropriate designation.

10. Give Clear Instructions

It is vital that small learning groups know exactly what is expected of them when they are formed. Unclear instructions will lead to an unproductive session. Whenever possible, write out specific, concise instructions on a card, chalkboard, flipchart or overhead transparency. Groups can then refer to the written instructions as often as necessary without needing the leader to verbalize them repeatedly.

11. Monitor Group Work

Small study or work groups, once formed and instructed, should not be left to themselves. The leader should monitor them—visit them occasionally, clarify instructions, assist with supplies, alert them as to the time remaining to work, etc. Such monitoring activity will assist groups in finishing on time.

12. Consider Permanent or Semi-Permanent Groups

While there is some value to study or work groups being formed at random each class session, permanent or semi-permanent groups meeting consistently from week to week seem to offer the best learning possibilities. In consistent groups, learners get to know one another better and are more likely to open themselves up to one another in the application of Bible principles.

13. Small Groups Must Share

One of the greater values of groups working individually is the sharing they do with the large group. A group which is given an assignment or task will be more productive if they know they will be sharing their findings or work with others in the classroom. Also, one group will benefit from hearing and seeing what another group has done. Plan to allow time for small groups to share their discoveries. NOTE: It is wise to call for groups to share in random order so that each group thinks, "We may be next, we had better pay attention."

Jr. High Sr. High

See explanation on page 14.

BUMPER STICKERS— (Badges or Buttons)

Purpose: Focus learners' attention and introduce the Bible study theme.

Materials
☐ Paper
☐ Scissors
☐ Felt pens
☐ Straight pins (for badges or buttons)
☐ Masking tape (for posting bumper stickers)

Procedure
1. Have table with materials in a prominent spot in your classroom or have chairs arranged in circles of 3-6 with supplies in the center.
2. Prepare (prior to class time) on chalkboard or overhead transparency the following directions:

BUMPER STICKER MANIA
Take paper and felt pen and create a bumper sticker that focuses on _____. (Example—the Christian's responsibility to care for and feed the poor and hungry.)
3. Learners share their bumper stickers by posting them around the room.

Variations
This same format can be used for campaign badges or buttons designed around a particular subject or theme. Provide straight pins so that learners can wear their badges or buttons during class time.

Example

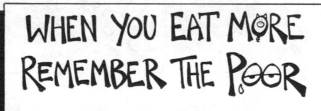

WHEN YOU EAT MORE REMEMBER THE POOR

Getting Started
Sample instructions for using bumper stickers in an Approach activity:
"Come on in and follow the instructions that you see posted. There are supplies all ready for you. When you have finished your work, post it on the wall."
Note: Post a sample bumper sticker on the wall for reference.

Sharing Bible Learning
"It looks like we have quite a creative group here today. Those of you who have not already done so, post your work. In today's class session we are going to be studying James 2:14-26 that provides us with some instruction regarding our attitudes and actions in response to those in need."

Jr. High   Sr. High

CARTOON STRIP

Purpose: Learners illustrate the main idea of a Scripture passage in the form of a cartoon strip.

Materials
☐ Bible for each learner
☐ Length of butcher paper and felt marker for each group of 3-6
☐ Clear instructions

Procedure
1. Move class into groups of three to six. Have each individual read and condense a pre-selected Scripture passage.
2. Learners share condensations with others in small group.
3. Have each group create a cartoon strip (on butcher paper) which illustrates the theme or principle from the studied passage of Scripture. Assure groups that simple stick figures and line drawings are satisfactory for their cartoons.
4. Have each group display and comment on their work. Use this discussion time to uncover the basic principles of the session.

Example

A DAY IN THE LIFE OF JIMMY CHRISTIAN   BY RON JONES AND GRANT SMITH

Getting Started
Sample instructions for using a cartoon strip in a Bible Exploration activity:

"We have just read Mark 12:28-34 and condensed the passage. Now I would like to have each group take their assigned passage and create a cartoon strip (on butcher paper) which illustrates the relationship between love for God and love for people. Be sure to portray practical outworkings of this relationship in your cartoon."

Sharing Bible Learning
Let's have each group display and comment on their cartoon strip."

"I think these cartoon strips have helped summarize the importance of the command to love God and people. They have uniquely illustrated some practical ways we demonstrate this love relationship."

ART ACTIVITIES

CHARTS

Purpose: Class members graphically display major points of information with charts that show relationships, categories or other qualities relevant to the lesson.

Materials
☐ Bibles for each learner
☐ Poster paper
☐ Felt pens
☐ Clear instructions

Procedure
1. Learners read pre-selected Scripture passage.
2. Move class into small groups, providing each with poster paper, pens and clear instructions. (In most cases the teacher should determine the headings and focus, assigning the group to gather information to complete the chart.)
3. Groups post and share their work with the class.

Variations
Learners can prepare charts as overhead transparencies or chalkboard presentations. Or, a chart format prepared on plain paper can be distributed for completion.

Example

	Characteristics of a Christian	Characteristics of a non-Christian	Differences between Christian and non-Christian
Eph. 2:1-10			
Phil. 3:1-11			
Col. 3:1-17			

Getting Started
Sample teacher instruction for using charts in a Bible Exploration activity:

"We have just read Galatians 1:11-24 where Paul was pointing to the change Christ had made in his life as another proof of the validity of his message to the Galatians. Now we are going to look at additional passages that relate some of the basic differences between being a Christian and not being a Christian. Each group will take one of the passages and prepare a chart like the sample posted."

Sharing Bible Learning
"Let's have the group that charted Philippians 3:1-11 share their work first."

"Some basic differences our charts show are: spiritual life versus spiritual death; trusting in Christ for salvation versus trusting in personal achievements. . . ."

27

ART ACTIVITIES

COAT OF ARMS

Purpose: Individuals illustrate specific aspects of their life or the life of a Bible character by drawing three or four sections on a shield as a coat of arms.

Materials
☐ Paper with outline of a simple coat of arms shield
☐ Clear instructions

Procedure
1. Provide each person with paper that has a coat of arms outline.
2. Have students draw an item in each of the four corners (see example).

Example

Most significant event in life from birth to 10.

Most significant event in life from 10 to to present.

Significant achievement or success of past year.

Happiest moment in an average day.

My Personal Coat of Arms

Getting Started
Sample teacher instructions for using coat of arms in an Approach activity:

"Each of us is a unique individual. Much of the way we are today can be traced back to a lifetime of varied experiences. Let's take five minutes to complete a coat of arms that will help explain something about each of us."

"In the left corner of your shield, sketch something that symbolizes a significant event from birth to 10 years; in the right corner, a significant event from 10 to the present time; in the lower left corner, a significant achievement or success from the past year; and in the lower right corner, the happiest moment in an average day. Be prepared to share your coat of arms with three others when you have finished."

Sharing Bible Learning
"Spend the next few minutes sharing your personal coats of arms with three others."

"In today's session we are going to be looking at a passage in the Gospel of Luke that deals with our personal uniqueness and God's ability to know us and work in and through us."

28

ART ACTIVITIES

FRIEZE/MURAL

Purpose: Learners work in small groups to illustrate the session theme, historic events or implications of Bible truth or event.

Materials
- ☐ Bible for each learner
- ☐ Butcher paper, felt pens
- ☐ Masking tape to post work

Procedure
1. Learners read pre-selected Scripture, looking for details and main idea(s).
2. Individuals or groups working together summarize the message of the passage.
3. Learners work in small groups to illustrate with pictures, stick figures, words or symbols a sequence of events covered in the Scripture studied.
4. Learners display and explain their work for the class. Teacher can then draw attention to the total picture illustrated by the frieze/mural.

Variations
1. Each small group can be assigned a section of the frieze. Prior to discussion, the various parts of the frieze can be put together in chronological order.
2. Make more elaborate friezes as a continuing project over a period of time.

Example

JONAH RUNS AWAY   STORM AT SEA   JONAH THROWN OVERBOARD   NINEVEH SPARED

Getting Started
Sample teacher instructions for using a frieze/mural in Bible Exploration:

"We have just read and summarized the message from the book of Jonah. Now I'd like each group to illustrate one chapter by making a frieze. A frieze is a picture story that traces events in their chronological order. It need not be elaborate; you can use simple pictures, stick figures and words. Be sure to include: your visual concept of the action as well as God's teaching on obedience and compassion as you see it in the passage. Write a brief 'Focus of the Passage' beneath your illustrations and be prepared to share your work with the class."

Sharing Bible Learning
"Let's have each group post their frieze chapter, and one member briefly share the frieze message with the class. The group that worked on chapter 1 is first."

"We can now see the complete story of Jonah and God's interaction in his life."

A
B
C

Jr. High   Sr. High

MONTAGE/COLLAGE

Purpose: That learners prepare an artistic composition which conveys a unified theme, made by combining several separate pictures.

Materials
- ☐ Old magazines, catalogues, newspapers
- ☐ Large sheets of paper or posterboard
- ☐ Glue/tape
- ☐ Scissors
- ☐ Clear instructions

Procedure
1. Learners read/ discuss the main ideas/ meaning of a predetermined Bible passage.
2. Learners work in small groups to create a montage to communicate the meaning of the passage. They do this by selecting pictures and words that illustrate the concepts represented in Scripture. Items are cut and arranged together to convey a unified idea or theme.
3. Groups post and share their work with the entire class.

Variation
A collage is similar to a montage; however, it is made of various materials such as wood, rope, paper or cloth and glued on a picture surface.

Example

Getting Started
Sample teacher instruction for using a montage in a Bible Exploration activity:

"We have just read Philippians 1:7-11 and discussed the implications. Now I would like you to imagine that the people with whom you are communicating cannot read. Using Philippians 1:7-11 as your source of ideas, find pictures that illustrate the concepts in this passage. Cut out the pictures and glue them onto your background to make a montage that communicates the kind of things Paul was saying about supportive fellowships in his letter to Philippi."

Sharing Bible Learning
"Let's have each group post their montage on the wall when they have it finished and share the message with the rest of the class."

"Our montages do a good job of communicating Paul's emphasis on the importance of believers' support and encouragement of one another."

WIRE SCULPTURE

Purpose: Focus learners' attention and introduce the theme for a particular Bible study session.

Materials
☐ Chenille wires (pipe cleaners)

Procedure
1. Have two or three chenille-covered wires on each chair as students arrive.
2. Prior to class, write clear instructions on a chalkboard or overhead transparency. The instructions need to explain that each person is to bend and twist his or her wires into a shape that is representative of the pre-determined theme of the session.
3. Allow three or four minutes for individuals to work and two to five minutes for them to show and explain their sculpture to each other.

Example

Getting Started
Sample instruction for using wire sculpture in an Approach activity:

"Daydream for a moment that you are wealthy enough to hire a personal servant—someone who would be available at all times to do whatever you wished. Now bend and twist your chenille-covered wires into a shape which represents what you would be most grateful to have a servant do for you."

Sharing Bible Learning
"We have seen a wide variety of tasks represented by some rather unique sculptures—mowing the lawn, taking out the trash, babysitting, cleaning your room, etc. In today's Bible study session we will be studying Mark 10:1-52 and the role of the Christian as a servant to others."

CREATIVE WRITING

ABRIDGED EDITION

Purpose: That learners condense the content of a passage of Scripture to its essential meaning.

Materials
☐ Bibles for each learner
☐ Writing paper
☐ Pens or pencils

Procedure
1. Learners read pre-selected passage of Scripture, looking for main idea(s).
2. Individuals or groups working together summarize the message of the passage.
3. Learners write their summary in as few words as possible.
4. Learners share their abridged editions with each other, focusing on main idea they want to emphasize.

Variations
1. Learners write their abridged editions in the form of telegrams, bumper stickers, slogans, etc.
2. Abridged editions or telegrams may be written on poster paper for classroom display.

Examples
Psalm 1:1-6 (*NIV*)
   1. Blessed is the man who does not walk in the counsel of the wicked or stand in the way of sinners or sit in the seat of mockers.
   2. But his delight is in the law of the Lord, and on his law he meditates day and night.
   3. He is like a tree planted by streams of water, which yields its fruit in season and whose leaf does not wither. Whatever he does prospers.
   4. Not so the wicked! They are like chaff that the wind blows away.
   5. Therefore the wicked will not stand in the judgment, nor sinners in the assembly of the righteous.
   6. For the Lord watches over the way of the righteous, but the way of the wicked will perish.

Abridged Edition of Psalm 1:1-6

"The godly person is happy and prosperous, but the wicked person is fruitless and destined for ruin."

Telegram Version of Psalm 1:1-6
GODLY PERSON SHUNS WICKED AND PROSPERS. UNGODLY FACE GOD'S JUDGMENT.

Getting Started

Sample teacher instructions for using abridged edition in a Bible Exploration activity:

"Turn in your Bibles to Psalm 1:1-6. Who would like to read this passage aloud for us?

"Let's write an abridged edition of this passage by condensing these six verses into one statement which expresses its essential meaning. Work in pairs to see if you can condense Psalm 1 into 20 words or less. Each pair letter your abridged edition on a large sheet of paper with a felt marker for display when we talk about them."

Sharing Bible Learning

"You've done a great job condensing Psalm 1 into several abridged editions which will help us get a grasp of its basic meaning. Let's have each pair post their abridged edition on the bulletin board, then one of you read your statement aloud and tell us why you phrased it as you did. Ken and Brad, will you be first?

"Each abridged edition has helped us see more clearly that Psalm 1 is a contrast between two kinds of people."

CREATIVE WRITING

ACROSTIC

Purpose: That learners express words and/or phrases relating to a specific Bible theme.

Materials
☐ Poster paper, butcher paper, writing paper or chalkboard
☐ Felt pens, pens, pencils or chalk

Procedure
1. Teacher letters a word or brief phrase vertically on a large sheet of paper.
2. Learners write words or phrases related to the theme horizontally on poster beginning with each letter of the vertical word(s).
3. When writing is completed, learners discuss many of the words or phrases written.

Variations
1. Acrostics can be written on overhead transparencies for projection by overhead projector.
2. Individual acrostics can be prepared for duplication on photocopier or mimeographs so each learner may complete his/her own individual acrostic.
3. Acrostics can be arranged into acrostic puzzles as described on page 100.

Examples

WALKING THE TALK
"**I** AM ONE"
TRUSTING THE HOLY SPIRIT
NEVER ALONE
EYEWITNESS OF GOD'S LOVE
SALVATION STORY
STEVE IS MY WITNESSING TARGET

Getting Started

Sample teacher instructions for using an acrostic in an Approach activity:

"We've been studying the life of Jesus Christ in class. Notice the large letters printed vertically on the chalkboard spelling 'JESUS.' I wonder how many words or phrases you can think of beginning with each of these five letters—J-E-S-U-S—which describe something about Jesus. For example, 'S' might stand for 'Son of God.' If you can think of a word or phrase, come take a piece of chalk and write it on the board beside the appropriate letter. Let's see if each one of us can contribute at least one word or phrase to our 'JESUS' acrostic."

Sharing Bible Learning

"We've almost run out of room on the chalkboard because you have all contributed some excellent words and phrases about Jesus. Now let's talk about some of them. Kristie, I saw you add the word 'exciting' beside the letter 'E.' Can you tell us something exciting about Jesus?

"With these thoughts about Jesus fresh in our minds, let's turn to Mark 10 in our Bibles and see what else we can learn."

CONTEMPORARY STORY/PARABLE

Purpose: That learners describe the events of a biblical narrative or principle in a contemporary setting.

Materials
☐ Bible for each learner
☐ Writing paper
☐ Pens or pencils

Procedure
1. Learners read pre-selected biblical narrative or passage to discover desired principles.
2. Individuals or groups write stories using contemporary settings and characters which parallel the biblical account and bring biblical principles into modern day focus.
3. Learners read their contemporary stories to each other and discuss the comparisons and contrasts with the biblical passage.

Variations
1. Contemporary stories may be written on poster paper and illustrated for classroom display.
2. Learners may conduct a newspaper search, looking for news or feature articles which illustrate biblical narratives or principles.
3. Contemporary stories may be written in the form of newspaper articles, television news scripts or radio reports.

Example
Contemporary story written from Luke 10:30-37, the good Samaritan.

There once was a kid named Terry who had a bad drug problem, had been expelled from school and kicked out of his home by his parents. He was hitch-hiking to another city when a carload of kids drove by and threw a beer bottle at him from the car, leaving a cut on his head. While Terry was standing by the road holding his head another car swerved toward him, forcing him to jump into the ditch and injuring his leg. A boy named Brad drove by and saw Terry lying in the ditch. He stopped his car and ran back to help him. Brad helped Terry into his car and drove him to the emergency hospital to receive medical attention. Then Brad took the injured boy to his home, gave him something to eat and let him sleep in his own room. Brad and his parents kept Terry until Terry's parents were willing to take him back. Terry is now attending school again, recovering from his drug problem and visiting the church where Brad and his family attend.

Getting Started
Sample teacher instructions for using the contemporary story in a Bible Exploration activity:

"We've seen from our discussion of the parable of the good Samaritan in Luke 10:30-37 that Jesus wanted His followers to express love even to those considered 'unlovable.' He illustrated that truth with a story which helped them understand. Imagine now that Jesus was present in our class today to illustrate that truth with a story *teenagers* could understand and identify with. What setting might He choose? What kind of characters might He use? Work in teams of three to write a brief contemporary story—5-8 sentences—illustrating for teens Jesus' concept of loving the 'unlovable.' Select for your story a setting and characters that would communicate to teens."

Sharing Bible Learning
"Which group would like to be first to read us your contemporary story?"

"What character in this story best illustrates the kind of love Jesus was talking about? Why?"

CREATIVE WRITING

CROSSWORD LISTING

Purpose: That learners identify key words and/or phrases in a passage of Scripture or lesson and list them in crossword puzzle form.

Materials
☐ Bible for each learner
☐ Graph paper with at least ¼ inch squares
☐ Pens or pencils

Procedure
1. Learners read pre-selected passage of Scripture and list the key words of the passage.
2. Individuals or groups arrange key words from Scripture passage in interlocking crossword fashion.
3. Learners show their crossword lists to each other while talking about the meaning of the key words they have listed.

Variations
1. Crossword listing is ideal for listing two *contrasting* lists from Scriptures—one list may be recorded horizontally and a contrasting list recorded vertically (see examples).
3. Crossword lists may be written on poster paper for classroom display.
4. Crossword puzzles—where learners fill in blanks of a crossword puzzle from written clues—is a learning activity which is described on page 102.

Examples
A crossword list of the fruit of the Spirit, Galatians 5:22,23 (*NIV*).

```
                    P
                    A                   P
           F A I T H F U L N E S S
                    I                   A
                    E                   C
        G E N T L E N E S S            E
        O               C
      J O Y             E
        D
  K I N D N E S S
        E                     L
        S E L F - C O N T R O L
        S                     V
                              E
```

A crossword list contrasting heavenly wisdom (horizontal) with earthly wisdom (vertical) from James 3:13-18 (*NIV*).

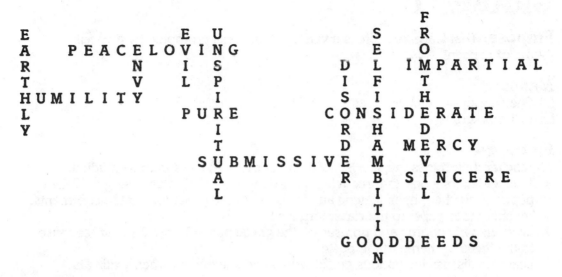

Getting Started

Sample teacher instructions for using crossword listing in a Bible Exploration activity:

"In James 3:13-18 we find a description of two kinds of wisdom—heavenly wisdom and earthly wisdom. Read this passage as a group and list all the words which describe heavenly wisdom in one column and all the words which describe earthly wisdom in another column. Then arrange your lists into a crossword puzzle format on the poster paper provided. List words describing heavenly wisdom horizontally on the puzzle and words describing earthly wisdom vertically on the puzzle."

Sharing Bible Learning

"Please post your crossword lists and let's identify the qualities of heavenly wisdom together by comparing the horizontal words on each of the lists. Brian, would you please read aloud from your group's crossword list the words describing heavenly wisdom?"

CREATIVE WRITING

GRAFFITI

Purpose: That learners express a variety of thoughts prompted by a specific theme or concept.

Materials
☐ Shelf paper or butcher paper
☐ Felt markers

Procedure
1. Teacher determines the specific focus or theme of the lesson to be studied.
2. Teacher letters a one-to-three word summary of the theme on a length of shelf paper or butcher paper, leaving ample space on the paper for written comments.
3. Teacher tapes paper to the classroom wall.
4. Learners write words and phrases on the graffiti poster based on their response to the focus or theme of the poster.
5. Learners discuss the various graffiti words and statements when writing is completed.

Variations
1. Graffiti writing can be done on chalkboard or overhead transparency.
2. The graffiti theme can be revealed to a portion of the class and withheld from another portion, with the graffiti poster being blank. The part of the class "in the know" writes theme-related graffiti statements on the poster while the other part of the class tries to guess the theme.

Example

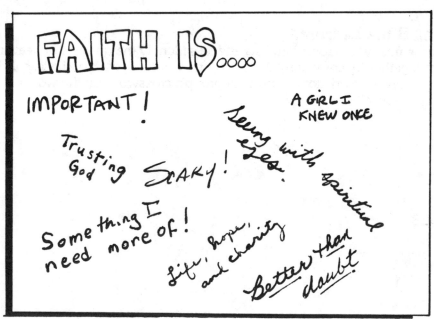

Getting Started

Sample teacher instructions for using graffiti in an Approach activity:

"You all noticed the big sheet of paper on the wall with the colorful words 'FAITH IS. . .' lettered on it. Faith is many things, and brings many thoughts to mind. What thoughts does faith bring to your mind? How would you complete that phrase, 'FAITH IS. . .'? Think about it for a moment, then take a felt marker from the table and add your graffiti thoughts on faith to our graffiti poster."

Sharing Bible Learning

"Let's talk about some of the things you have written on the graffiti poster. Who wrote this statement, 'Sometimes blind trust'? Would you tell us in a sentence what you were thinking about as you wrote that statement?

"I've enjoyed talking about these concepts of faith we have on the graffiti poster. Now let's look into God's Word and see what God has to say about faith. Turn to Hebrews 11. . ."

LETTER WRITING

Purpose: That learners express their personal experiences or feelings in response to exploring a Bible principle.

Materials
☐ Bible for each learner
☐ Writing paper
☐ Pens or pencils
☐ Envelopes and stamps (optional)

Procedure
1. Learners explore pre-selected section of Scripture and discuss the principles involved.
2. Learners write letters addressed to a Bible character or friend as a personal response to the Scripture.
3. Learners discuss their letters with one another and/or mail their letters to the addressee.

Variations
1. Letter writing may be used as a Bible Exploration activity by having learners take the identity of a Bible character and write his/her account or impression of a Bible event.
2. Letters may be written on poster paper for classroom display.
3. Learners may be instructed to write letters of response to Scripture and personal commitment and address them to themselves. Teachers may hold letters for a time and then return them to the learners in person or by mail so learners may evaluate their response after a period of time has elapsed.

Examples
Here is a letter of personal response and commitment written to Abraham concluding a study of obedience from Genesis 22:1-19.

Dear Abraham,
You really taught me something today about obedience. I could hardly believe my eyes when I read that you almost killed your son Isaac because God told you to do so. Did you know God was testing you to see if you would obey or chicken out? If so, did you begin to wonder or get scared when you took out the knife just before God spoke to you?

You learned to obey God in a BIG test. I'm still learning to obey God in some little things like not cheating and telling the truth to my parents.

Thank you for your example, Mr. Abraham. If God could help you obey Him in the tough situation we studied today, I think He could help me in the areas of my life where I'm still learning to be faithful and obedient.

Sincerely, Chuck.

Here is a letter written as a Bible Exploration activity for Genesis 22:1-19. It is a letter written as Isaac might have written it to a friend, describing the event of the sacrifice.

Dear Reuben,

Remember last week when I wrote and told you that Dad and I had a special backpacking trip planned to Mount Moriah? You won't believe it, but I thought for a few minutes it was going to be my *last* trip anywhere!

Dad said the main part of the trip was to offer a sacrifice to the Lord. But when we got to the place of the sacrifice, I asked him where the lamb was. "God will provide the lamb," he said. It was really strange because I didn't see any animals around anywhere. But Dad is a wise man, and I figured he knew what he was talking about.

At the top of the mountain we built the altar—but still no lamb. Before I knew what was happening, Dad was tying my hands behind my back and tying my legs together. Then he lifted me up and laid me on the altar! Boy, was I getting scared— Dad wasn't making any sense. I know he loves me, but here he was getting ready to sacrifice me to the Lord!

Then I saw the knife. I was just ready to let out a scream when God's voice from heaven called my dad by name, told him not to sacrifice me and pointed him to a ram caught in the bushes. I was never more thankful to see an animal in my life.

On the way home, we had a long talk about obedience to God. I learned a lot from my dad that day. I learned that God provides for those who obey Him.

Your friend, Isaac.

Getting Started

Sample teacher instructions for using letter writing in a Conclusion/Decision activity:

"We have seen in Genesis 22:1-19 how Abraham obeyed God even when he thought God was going to have him sacrifice his son Isaac. We have also discussed that obedience for believers today is not always the most convenient thing to do, but it is always the right thing to do. Imagine that we could send a letter to Abraham and express to him our thoughts and feelings about what we learned about obedience today through his example. What would you write about? Let's each take a sheet of paper and write a letter to Abraham saying something about what we learned about obedience to God from his experience."

Sharing Bible Learning

"Just before we close in prayer, are there two or three of you who would volunteer to read your letters to the class? I'm sure we will find several areas of obedience to God that are common to many of us. Who would be first?"

CREATIVE WRITING

LIST

Purpose: That learners itemize specific points of information or thought on a given Scripture passage or theme.

Materials
☐ Writing paper
☐ Pens or pencils
☐ Poster paper and felt pens (optional)

Procedure
1. Learners are presented with a pre-selected block of information—passage of Scripture, theme, etc.
2. Individuals or groups itemize specific points of information from the information presented.
3. Learners list their itemized points on paper.
4. Learners report their lists to the class.

Variations
1. Lists may be written on poster paper with felt markers for classroom display.
2. Lists may be presented in a number of creative ways, using other methods of expression (i.e. recipes, bumper stickers, interview, crossword listing, etc.).

Examples
The following is a list which represents qualities an overseer in the church *is* and *is not* supposed to possess, from 1 Timothy 3:1-7 (*NIV*):

An overseer is to be. . .	An overseer is not to be. . .
above reproach	given to much wine
husband of one wife	violent
temperate	quarrelsome
self-controlled	lover of money
respectable	recent convert
hospitable	
able to teach	
manage family well	
obedient children	
good reputation	

The following is a list teens compiled in response to the question, "What are the barriers teens face today in establishing consistent personal Bible study patterns?"

TV
peer pressure
lack of personal discipline
overcrowded schedule
too much homework

lack of commitment to study the Word
family pressures
Satan's interference
lack of Bible study guidelines and resources

Getting Started

Sample teacher instructions for using a list in a Bible Exploration activity.

"We have discussed from 2 Timothy 3:16,17 the importance of being involved in the Word of God, and we have agreed that each believer should establish a personal pattern for Bible study. But we also know that there are several things that keep us from establishing this pattern. For example, the television is sometimes an interruption in our pattern—we choose to watch a program on TV which appeals to us instead of spending time studying God's Word. What are some of the other barriers teens face today in establishing consistent personal Bible study patterns? Work together in groups of three to list on your worksheet other things which keep us from Bible study."

Sharing Bible Learning

"Let's compare our lists now, with each group sharing one of the barriers they listed. We'll continue taking one idea per group until we have compiled a composite list. I will write them on the chalkboard. Debi, what is one barrier your group discussed?"

MEMO

Purpose: That learners express personal response to a Bible study theme with a brief, written instruction to themselves.

Materials
☐ Office memo blanks (real or simulated)
☐ Pens or pencils

Procedure
1. Individual learners identify one personal response they need to make to a Scripture passage or theme.
2. Learners write a brief directive to themselves in the form of an office memo outlining how they will apply their personal response.
3. Volunteers read their memos to the class and discuss their intended responses.

Variations
1. Memos may be written on poster paper for classroom display.
2. Memos may be enclosed in self-addressed stamped envelopes to be mailed to learners at the end of the month, quarter or term.
3. Memos may be exchanged among the learners to serve as prayer requests—each learner praying for another learner through the week concerning the response written on the memo.

Example

> MEMO TO: *Me*
>
> MEMO FROM: *Me*
>
> MEMO SUBJECT: *Temptation at the mini-market*
>
> Since it is important to "flee the evil desires of youth," you better stay away from the magazine section at the mini-market. There are too many magazines on the rack which will fill your mind with the wrong kinds of pictures and words.

Getting Started

Sample teacher instructions for using the memo in a Conclusion and Decision activity:

"We have seen from James chapter 1 that temptation comes from our own ungodly desires, and we have talked about several of the temptations that teen-aged boys face today. If you decided today to do what Paul told Timothy to do in 2 Timothy 2:22, 'Flee the evil desires of youth, and pursue righteousness, faith, love and peace,' what is one temptation you would turn away from this coming week and how would you turn away from it? Take an office memo form and write yourself a memo giving yourself a two- to three-sentence instruction on how you will respond to our lesson in the coming week."

Sharing Bible Learning

"The memo you have written to yourself may be too personal to share with the rest of the class. But we will take a few moments now to allow for some of you to volunteer to read your memo to the class. You will be surprised at how helpful you might be to someone else to follow their own memo if they hear what you have decided to do in obedience to God's Word. Do we have any volunteers who will read?"

CREATIVE WRITING

NEWSPAPER STORY

Purpose: That learners report the details of a biblical event, using the format of a newspaper article.

Materials
☐ Bible for each learner
☐ Writing paper
☐ Pens or pencils

Procedure
1. Learners read pre-selected passage of Scripture outlining a biblical event.
2. Individuals or groups working together write the account of the event as it might have appeared in a newspaper at the time. News stories should supply answers to the journalistic questions "who, what, when, where, how and why?"
3. Learners share their newspaper stories with each other.

Variations
1. Newspaper stories may be written on poster paper for classroom display.
2. Newspaper stories may be presented in the format of a television or radio news program (see "TV/Radio Show," page 78).
3. Newspaper stories may be written from the perspective of believing or unbelieving reporters.
4. The newspaper format can be utilized to summarize the historical events of a series of lessons. In addition to news stories, the newspaper might include editorials, a sports section, advertisements, and even want ads.
5. Newspaper headlines may be written instead of news stories to summarize several biblical events.

Example
The following news story reports the event found in 2 Kings 2:23-25:

42 TEENS MAULED BY BEARS

Prophet jeered, calls down curse

BETHEL (IP) — Forty-two rowdy teenagers, who had been shouting obscenities and insults at the prophet Elisha beside Bethel Boulevard, were severely injured yesterday when two angry bears charged out of the forest and attacked them. Witnesses said that the bears appeared after Elisha, an itinerant prophet traveling through the region, called down a curse in the name of the Lord on the crowd of rebellious youths. The injured were taken to Bethel Community Hospital where several remain in critical condition.

Apparently a growing mob of teens had followed Elisha along the highway for several miles, making fun of the prophet's baldness. At one point Elisha stopped, turned and looked at them, and then uttered a curse upon them for their rebellion and disrespect. When the bears emerged from the woods, the youths scattered in fear. But many were frozen in terror and became easy prey for the beasts.

Elisha, who was unharmed during the incident, continued on to Mt. Carmel and was unavailable for comment.

Getting Started

Sample teacher instructions for using a newspaper story in a Bible Exploration activity:

"Turn to 2 Kings 2:23 in your Bibles. Who would volunteer to read verses 23, 24 and 25 for us? Thank you, Roger. Let's follow along silently as Roger reads.

"Imagine that you were a reporter for the Bethel Banner, a newspaper from the town of Bethel near the scene of our Scripture passage. You have just received the information about Elisha and the rebellious youths as recorded in 2 Kings 2:23-25. Write a newspaper story describing the event as it might have appeared in the imaginary Bethel Banner. Remember, a news story must answer these questions: who, what, when, where, why and how? Work as a small group to write a news story and letter your final composition on a sheet of poster paper for class sharing later. You have 10 minutes to work. Your story should be from three to five sentences in length."

Sharing Bible Learning

"Let's have each group post its news story on the wall, and a member of each group read the news story for the class. Bonnie, let's start with your group."

Jr. High   Sr. High

OPEN-ENDED STORY

Purpose: That learners use scriptural principles to solve a specific true-to-life dilemma as presented in an unfinished story.

Materials
☐ Mimeographed or photocopied worksheets containing the text of the open-ended story
☐ Pens or pencils

Procedure
1. Learners discuss scriptural principles which will be involved in the open-ended story.
2. Individuals or groups working together read the unfinished story and then write a conclusion to the story, based on their application of scriptural principles to the story situation.
3. Learners share their open-ended story completions with each other.

Variations
1. Open-ended story completions may be written on poster paper for classroom display.
2. Learners may act out their written story completions for the rest of the class.
3. Roleplay may be substituted for open-ended story completion with the same goals being accomplished (see "Roleplay," page 74).
4. Learners may complete open-middle stories in which a problem is the beginning and there is a statement of resolution at the end (the problem may or may not have been solved). Learners write the middle of the story, which describes what was done to bring about the concluding statement.

Example
This open-ended story is followed by one learner's completion:

"When Sue came home, bringing her friend Fran along, she planned to ask her mother if she could go bicycle riding. Fran had a new 10-speed bicycle she wanted to show to Sue. Some older boys were going to meet them at the park so they could all ride around together. But Sue's mother wasn't home. She had left a note asking Sue to stay at home and start dinner. Fran urges Sue to come out and ride bikes anyway. She tells her she can probably get home in time to start supper. What will Sue do?"

One learner's story completion:

Sue thought about her options: she probably *could* go riding and be home in time to start dinner; she could go to Fran's and see the new bike but not go riding; she could leave a note explaining her situation to her mother. But Sue decided that she would not be honoring her mother in the situation if she left home without talking to her mother first. So she asked Fran if she would mind bringing her new bike to Sue's house to show her on the way to the park. If Sue's mother returned home or phoned before Fran returned, Sue would ask her permission to ride for a while. Otherwise, she would remain home and arrange another time to ride with Fran.

Getting Started

Sample teacher instructions for using the open-ended story in a Bible Exploration activity:

"We have been discussing Ephesians 6:1-3 and the guidelines we discovered there for the relationship of teens to their parents. We have also talked about what it means to *honor* parents. Let's look now at a situation in which a teenager had an opportunity to honor her mother. On your worksheet you see the first part of a story. Please follow along as I read this paragraph aloud. (Read paragraph.) Notice that the story is open-ended. It is purposely left incomplete so that we could write an ending for it. Let's take the next five minutes working individually to write an end to the story. The learners on the left side of the room should complete the story showing Sue applying the principles we discovered in today's Scripture study. The people on the right side of the room should complete the story showing Sue ignoring the principles we have talked about. At the end of five minutes, we will compare story completions."

Sharing Bible Learning

"I want to invite several of you to share your story completion within your small group. After each person reads his or her story, talk about it for a few minutes using these questions: How did Sue honor or dishonor her mother in the completed story? What are some ways Fran might have responded to Sue's choice?"

Jr. High   Sr. High

PARAPHRASE

Purpose: That learners rewrite Scripture verses in their own words, making the Bible more understandable to them.

Materials
☐ Bible for each learner
☐ Writing paper
☐ Pens or pencils

Procedure
1. Direct learners' attention to one or more pre-selected passages of Scripture.
2. Individuals or groups working together read the passage and then rewrite the passage in their own words, clarifying and personalizing its meaning to them.
3. Learners share their paraphrased verses with each other.

Variations
1. Paraphrased verses may be written on poster paper for classroom display.
2. Learners may be given several verses on a selected theme and asked to paraphrase those verses into a paragraph explaining the meaning of the verses and theme.
3. Learners may be asked to rewrite verses in words which a child could understand—forcing them to simplify the concept in the passage into elementary vocabulary.

Examples
Romans 12:1: "Therefore, I urge you, brothers, in view of God's mercy, to offer your bodies as living sacrifices, holy and pleasing to God—which is your spiritual worship."

Romans 12:1, paraphrased: "Since God has been so full of mercy to us, brothers in the Lord, it's really important that we give ourselves to him sacrificially—not as dead animal sacrifices, but as breathing, moving, active sacrifices which are concerned with doing what God wants. When it comes right down to it, living sacrificially is what real worship is all about."

Paraphrase of several verses of Scripture explaining salvation (Romans 3:23; 5:8; John 1:12; 3:16; Romans 10:13): "I have sinned and do not measure up to God's standards. But, God showed His great love for me while I was still a sinner, by sending Christ to die for me. And if I receive Him, God will give the power to become His child. All I have to do is trust God and believe in Christ. When I believe, I will live forever, because whoever calls out to God will be saved!"

Getting Started
Sample teacher instructions for using a paraphrase in a Bible Exploration activity:

"Turn in your Bibles to Romans 12:1. Who would like to read this verse aloud for us? Thank you, Roger. Read for us while we follow along.

"Let's consider some of the key words in this verse. Why did Paul call his readers 'brothers'? Were they his flesh-and-blood relatives, or is he referring to another relationship?

"Now that we have talked through several of the key words in this verse, let's see if we can paraphrase it—that means to write it in our own words—so that the verse is more understandable to us. Take a sheet of paper and a pencil, and rewrite the verse in your own words, trying to make it as understandable as possible based on what we discussed. You will have four minutes to work on your paraphrase."

Sharing Bible Learning

"I see that most everyone is just completing their paraphrase, and I know that your good work will help us understand Paul's message in this verse even more. Who would like to be first to read their paraphrase to us?"

CREATIVE WRITING

PRAYER

Purpose: That learners express a personal prayer request or praise to God in written form.

Materials
☐ Writing paper
☐ Pens or pencils

Procedure
1. Learners discuss a pre-selected Scripture passage or theme and relate their discoveries to their personal lives.
2. Individual learners express their personal response to God by writing a prayer or praise based on the Bible study message they discovered.
3. Volunteers read their prayers aloud to God in the presence of other class members.

Variations
1. Prayers may be written in the form of letters to God ("Dear God . . . Sincerely, Pam").
2. Learners may be asked to take their written prayers home and place them in a conspicuous location so they may read their prayers to God each day during the week.
3. Learners may study Bible characters and events and write prayers or praises the Bible characters might have offered in their circumstances.
4. Learners may be asked to write collects—one-line prayers which help each learner zero in on specific changes he wants to make as a result of the lesson.

Examples
The following written prayer is based on a lesson from Matthew 5:13 and the theme of believers being the salt of the world.

"Jesus, you have said that I am the salt of the earth. We talked about what salt does—helps the flavor of food and acts as a preservative. I need your help to make me an even 'saltier' influence on the world around me. I want to add flavor to the lives of those who live around me and go to school with me. The flavor of your love. I don't want to be like the salt that has lost its 'saltiness.' I ask you now to increase my flavor content as the salt of my part of the world. And I ask this in Jesus' name. Amen."

The following collect is based on the same lesson: "Dear Lord, flavor my life with your love and strength so I can do likewise to others. Amen."

Getting Started
Sample teacher instructions for using prayer in a Conclusion and Decision activity:

"We have read that Jesus calls us the salt of the earth and we have discovered some of the qualities and purposes of salt, helping us to understand what Jesus was referring to. As we have studied today, I wonder if you have become aware of some areas of your life which you need to talk to the Lord about regarding the theme of your 'saltiness' in your world. In these closing moments of our lesson, I invite each of you to take a sheet of paper and write a prayer to God based on today's lesson. You might want to thank Him for the privilege of being salt. You might want to ask Him to help you be a more influential Christian in some areas. Write your prayer or praise on the paper, and then we will offer our prayers to God before we dismiss."

Sharing Bible Learning

"Just before we dismiss, I want to invite several of you to volunteer to read aloud your prayer or praise to God, and we will agree with you as you pray. You are not required to read aloud, but you may find it helpful and strengthening to you to express your hearts' prayer aloud to God while we are all in an attitude of prayer. Who would like to begin?"

STATEMENT COMPLETION

Purpose: That learners express their ideas or opinions on a lesson topic in response to an incomplete statement.

Materials
☐ Writing paper
☐ Pens or pencils

Procedure
1. Learners are introduced to an incomplete statement related to the lesson topic and asked to complete the statement in writing as it seems most appropriate to them.
2. Learners share their statement completions with each other and use their discussion to launch them into further study.

Variations
1. Incomplete statements may be written on the chalkboard or a large sheet of poster paper so that learners may add their statement completions in graffiti fashion.
2. Learners may be given a list of pre-selected completions from which they must choose one which best represents their personal response.
3. Incomplete statements may be written on chalkboard, overhead transparency or flipchart for introduction to learners, or they may be mimeographed or photocopied on worksheets for distribution to individual learners.

Examples
The following incomplete statements introduce a lesson on wisdom from James 1:5-7:

The wisest man or woman I have ever know personally is_____
_____.

He/she impressed me that way because _____
_____.

The following incomplete statement, with multiple choice completions, concludes a lesson on wisdom from James 1:5-7:
The area of my life in which I need to ask for God's wisdom most right now is:
_____my home life, because_____.
_____my school life, because _____.
_____my social life, because _____.
_____my spiritual life, because _____.
_____ my _____ life, because _____.

Getting Started
Sample teacher instructions for using a statement completion in an Approach activity:

56

"Have you ever been called a 'wise guy'? That's a phrase we use to describe someone who is arrogant or mouthy. Today we want to begin our lesson by thinking about some persons who are really wise. Notice the two incomplete statements on the chalkboard, 'The wisest man or woman I have ever known personally is' and 'He/she impressed me that way because.' Who comes to mind when you think of wise persons and why? Perhaps a teacher, relative or friend fits that description. Take your sheet of paper and complete those two statements—first with the name or description of a wise man or woman you have known or presently know personally, and second with an explanation of why you identify them as such."

Sharing Bible Learning

"Let's take a few moments to share our statement completions with others. Nudge your neighbor—that means visit with the person sitting next to you—and read your statement completions to each other. If you like, you might want to add a couple of sentences of explanation to what you have written. You and your partner have a total of one minute—thirty seconds each—to exchange information on your wisest man or woman.

"We've enjoyed thinking and talking about wise people we know or have known. Now let's look into God's Word to see what else we can learn about wisdom. Turn in your Bibles to James 1:5-7."

WRITTEN RESPONSE

Purpose: That learners express in writing opinions, ideas or conclusions provoked by one or more written, audio and/or visual sources.

Materials
- ☐ Writing paper
- ☐ Pens or pencils
- ☐ Item to provoke response

Procedure
1. Learners are introduced to a resource designed to produce a response (i.e. a passage of Scripture, a statement, a picture, a demonstration, a film, a recording, a monologue or sermon, etc.).
2. Learners write their personal responses to what they have seen and/or heard.
3. Learners share their written responses with each other.

Variations
1. Learners may be directed to write their responses in a certain number of words to encourage conciseness.
2. Written responses may be lettered on poster paper for classroom display.
3. Written responses may be produced in the form of letters, songs, poetry, prose, depending on the subject matter.
4. Written responses may be easily started by giving learners an incomplete statement to provoke their response.

Examples

> Read the following verse carefully. Then write your personal response to the verse in the space below in 25 words or less.
>
> 'If you forgive anyone his sins, they are forgiven; if you do not forgive them, they are not forgiven" (Jesus, John 20:23).
>
> *Power to forgive sins given by Jesus to man?! Power to hold people unforgiven?! Incredible! I wonder what Jesus really meant.*

Select one of the responses below which most closely represents your personal response to the film we have viewed. Then write one to two sentences explaining your response.

Praise the Lord!
Right on!
So-so!
Ho-hum!
Ouch!
Yuk!

Getting Started

Sample teacher instructions for using written response in a Bible Exploration activity:

"Our Bible study today takes us to a very interesting, and sometimes controversial, passage of Scripture. Before we get into the details, I want you to respond to the verse just as it is, just as you read it. Your worksheet instructs you to read John 20:23 to yourself and write your personal response in 25 words or less. You have two minutes to complete the assignment. Then we will talk about your responses and the details of the verse."

Sharing Bible Learning

"I noticed some of you struggling with your response, and that's okay. I struggle with my response to Scripture, too. But I am interested to hear how some of you responded to this thought-provoking verse. We're not looking for 'right' or 'wrong' answers here. We want to share our personal response to what Jesus said. Who would be brave enough to stand and read your written response? Kitty, go right ahead.

"I am impressed with the variety of responses you have shared—all of them very thoughtful and well written. Now let's get into the Scripture together and see if we can discover together what Jesus was driving at with this provocative statement."

AGREE-DISAGREE

Purpose: To stimulate interest in a topic by proposing a series of purposefully controversial statements on a given subject. Class members indicate whether they agree or disagree with the statements and why.

Materials
☐ A handout sheet, flipchart or chalkboard on which a series of statements is written

Procedure
1. Teacher asks students to read statements and determine if they agree or disagree.
2. Teacher reads statements aloud and asks students who agree to raise hands; then students who disagree to do the same.
3. Teacher calls attention to a statement on which opinion was divided and asks someone who agreed to tell why. Then someone who disagreed may speak. Allow several to speak for each side until differing positions have been clarified.
4. Continue this procedure with other statements as time allows.
5. Conclude the activity by affirming the group for honestly disagreeing without becoming disagreeable. Then lead group to Scripture passage to be studied.

Variations
1. Students may be asked to stand if they agree and to remain seated if they disagree.
2. All of group may be asked to stand. Those agreeing go to one side of room and the others to the other side, with "undecideds" in the middle.
3. The group may be asked to divide on the basis of "strongly agree," "moderately agree," "strongly disagree," and "moderately disagree."
4. After the group has been divided, they may try to convince the others of their position. Students may change sides at any time during such discussion.

Examples
● Christian kids should not be close friends with non-Christians.
● Parents have the right to read notes they find in your room.
● Popularity is the most important thing to most kids.

DISCUSSION ACTIVITIES

BRAINSTORMING

Purpose: To suggest as many ideas as possible on a given subject or problem with no evaluation made until all ideas are presented.

Materials
☐ Chalkboard, flipchart, large sheet of paper on which to record ideas
☐ Chalk, felt pen

Procedure
1. Announce that the group is going to brainstorm for five minutes (generally a short time of three to five minutes works best).
2. Instruct the learners that in brainstorming the idea is to come up with as many ideas as possible in the shortest time with no one evaluating an idea.
3. Assign someone in each group, or in the large group, to write down all the suggestions.
4. Announce the subject matter and begin timing.

Variations
1. Brainstorming works best in small groups of at least four to six persons but may be used in smaller groups.
2. After the brainstorming is concluded, some evaluation may be made of the various suggestions, depending upon the purpose for the brainstorming.

Examples
1. What are the characteristics of an ideal parent? child?
2. What are some of the ways we "trust in God"?
3. What is God like?
4. What are the characteristics of a Christian?
5. How many ways can we witness?
6. Come up with a list of objections people may have to the gospel.
7. Think of at least five practical things that students your age could do around the church.

A
B
C

Jr. High   Sr. High

BUZZ GROUPS

Purpose: To allow small groups to discuss a given subject for a brief period of time.

Materials
☐ Paper and pencils for notetaking
☐ A written statement of the subject to be discussed

Procedure
1. Small groups of four to six are formed in a circle.
2. A written statement of the subject to be discussed is handed out.
3. A time limit is set for the discussion—usually 3 to 20 minutes.
4. A recorder is chosen to record the group's results.

Variations
1. There are a host of variations that can be used with this format.
   • It can be used like the brainstorming session to develop some ways of coping with a problem, describing a concept or subject, or developing a project.
   • It can be used to study a particular Scripture to discover a meaning, list items, or develop an application.
2. Comparisons between the results from each group can be valuable in the development of workable ideas, in-depth Bible study, setting of priorities, or application of Scripture to life situations.

Examples
1. Make a list of five main areas of temptation kids your age have. Be prepared to share them with the group.
2. Read John 1:1-14. Come up with a list of things that God the Father or God the Son did. Then make a list of possible responses from man.
3. Tell why cheating is, or is not, harmful.

DISCUSSION ACTIVITIES

CIRCLE RESPONSES

Purpose: To engage each student in the discussion and participation in the lesson.

Materials
☐ Sheet of butcher paper, chalkboard, flipchart on which is written question, statement or verse(s) of Scripture

Procedure
1. The teacher calls the students' attention to the question, statement or verse(s).
2. Each learner is asked to respond.
3. This works best if the learners are sitting in a circle.
4. No one may speak a second time until all have spoken once.

Variations
1. If the group is large, smaller circles (4-8) of learners may be used.
2. When several circles are formed, different questions or statements may be used in each group and a report made on the general consensus in each group.
3. A listening team may be appointed in a group to be prepared to summarize the consensus of the group.

Examples
What was Christ's greatest miracle and why?

What was Christ's greatest statement and why?

Why did Christ have such a short ministry?

Why might you consider Jesus a rebel?

Of the events in Jesus' life here on earth, which was the most significant to you and why?

Which one characteristic of Jesus would you most seek or identify with and why?

What do you think Christ was doing from age 12 to age 30?

Why might someone decline Jesus' invitation to "Come, be my disciple"?

What was the second most significant event in the life of Christ? Why?

What impresses you most as to how Christ conducted Himself?

What was the most important moment in the lives of Christ's disciples? Why?

NEIGHBOR NUDGE

Purpose: To encourage participation by all the learners and to stimulate their interest in the coming lesson.

Materials
☐ Large sheet of paper, chalkboard, flipchart
☐ Felt marker for writing on paper or chalk for board

Procedure
1. Have everyone find a neighbor and get acquainted. Ask those without partners to raise their hands so they can find a neighbor.
2. A question or statement is placed on the chalkboard or other paper.
3. Learners are asked to discuss it with their neighbor (groups of two) for two minutes (or a limited time).

Variations
1. Circle response may be used in groups of three. Ask everyone to stand up. Then ask participants to be seated as soon as they have formed a group of three.
2. Teacher may ask a few of the groups to tell the class what they discovered, learned or agreed upon.

Examples
● Any of the agree-disagree (see page 60) or circle-response (see page 63) type questions are suitable for neighbor nudge.

PICTURE OR STATEMENT RESPONSE

Purpose: To focus attention on a particular object or subject and to encourage participation of learners.

Materials
☐ A picture or a written statement
☐ Sheets of paper for each learner
☐ Extra pencils

Procedure
1. Write a statement on the chalkboard or other material or place the picture in a prominent position.
2. Ask each learner to examine the picture or read the statement.
3. Ask each learner to write a one-sentence reaction or response.
4. Ask for volunteers to share what they wrote down.

Variations
1. The written statements can be shared in groups or by neighbor nudging.
2. A general discussion can follow with each person contributing something.

Examples
1. Many different pictures (illustrations or cartoons) might be used, including both secular and religious, depending upon the content of the lesson. A picture of Jesus on the shore, with His disciples in a boat fishing, might lead into the story in John 21:1-14.
2. Magazine ads or photos might be used to stimulate thought about values—for instance, "What does this ad try to say will happen to you if you use this product? What do you think Jesus would say about this?"
3. A statement like this might be made:
   "The values that you die by should be the values that you live by." What does this mean to you? Is it true? Why or why not?
4. Another statement might be:
   "Even though God forgives our sins, we are never really free from our past sin."

Jr. High   Sr. High

ACT OUT SCRIPTURE

Purpose: That learners identify with the experiences of Bible characters by dramatizing biblical narratives.

Materials
☐ Bible for each learner
☐ Necessary props

Procedure
1. Learners are directed to a pre-selected biblical narrative involving two or more Bible characters.
2. Learners are assigned the roles of Bible characters in the narrative. (Sometimes learners also take the roles of inanimate objects in the narrative such as trees, idols, etc.)
3. Learners study the narrative, becoming acquainted with the action and each character's role.
4. Learners present the narrative, simulating the action and reading or paraphrasing the dialogue between the characters.

Variations
1. In a narrative with little or no dialogue, learners may carry out the action of a biblical narrative while an assigned reader reads the narrative aloud.
2. Scriptural narratives may be acted out using contemporary settings and paraphrased contemporary dialogue (see Example A).
3. Two or more small groups may act out different segments of the same biblical narrative in chronological order.
4. Learners may act out a biblical narrative to a point of decision by a main character. Learners then act out alternative courses of action the character might have taken (see Example B).

Examples
Example A: The following dialogue represents a contemporary dramatization of Jesus and the rich young man from Matthew 19:16-22.

Christian teen: Pastor, please tell me what good things I can do to please God.

Pastor: If you want to please God, just follow the basic instructions of the Bible.

Christian teen: Exactly which 'basic instructions' are you referring to, Pastor?

Pastor: Read the Bible, attend church regularly, obey your parents. You know, the basics.

Christian teen (arrogantly): Well, Pastor, I'm doing real well on those. Aren't there just one or two things I might have missed?

Pastor: If you really want to please God, take the money you have been saving for a new stereo and pay your unsaved friend's way to camp. That will really please God.

Christian teen (dejectedly walking away): Maybe I better just stick with the basics.

Example B: Learners act out the dialogue between Jesus and the rich young man from Matthew 19:16-22 to the point where Jesus says, "Go, sell your possessions and give to the poor, . . . Then come, follow me" (Matthew 19:21). Then have learners act out alternative courses of action the rich young man might have taken in response to Jesus' instruction (e.g., argued with him about the validity of such a requirement, obediently followed through with Jesus' instruction, etc.).

Getting Started

Sample teacher instructions for using act out Scripture in a Bible Exploration activity:

"Today we are going to look at the account of Jesus and the rich young man in a different and exciting way. I would like our class to work in two groups—one group working on Matthew 19:16-22, the rich young man and Jesus, and one group working on Matthew 19:23-30, Jesus' discussion with His disciples about the event. Group one, would you study verses 16-22 and be prepared to act out that section for us? Group two, would you do the same with verses 23-30? In each group, volunteers take the roles of the characters involved and dramatize the action of the passage. You have five minutes to prepare your dramatization."

Sharing Bible Learning

"As I visited each group while you were working, I could tell that you were really putting yourself into the skin of your assigned characters. I can't wait to see your presentations. Group one, will you present your rendition of verses 16-22 for us?

"Thank you for a good job of helping us see the action in this passage. Before we move on to group two, let's talk about what we saw. How did the rich young man respond to Jesus' instructions? What are some other ways he might have responded?

"Group two, we're ready to see what you have done with verses 23-30.

"Thank you. Another helpful presentation. How did the disciples respond to Jesus' interaction with the rich young man? What are some other ways they might have responded?"

IN-BASKET

Purpose: That learners spontaneously act out possible responses to additional suggestions introduced during the course of a roleplay.

Materials
☐ Written roleplay assignments
☐ Written in-basket assignments

Procedure
1. Roleplay and setting assignments are explained to learners (see "Roleplay" on page 74).
2. As learners participate in the roleplay, they are given written directions of assigned responses they must act out spontaneously as the roleplay continues.
3. Learners discuss the attitudes and actions expressed during the in-basket exercise in the light of scriptural principles previously explored.

Variations
1. In-basket responses may be written on a slip of paper and drawn at random by the participating roleplayers.
2. In-basket responses may be suggested to the roleplayers by the viewing learners.

Examples
After the presentation of biblical principles for witnessing, and a discussion of some methods whereby Christian teens may share their faith with their friends, a roleplay/in-basket activity like the following may be used to dramatize some methods in real life situations.

Roleplay assignment: A Christian girl is having a Coke with two of her unchristian friends who are inquiring why she spends so much time at church and not as much time with them in their less-than-Christian pursuits. As the three learners spontaneously act out the situation, the following in-basket assignments may be given to, or drawn by, the respective roleplayers:

Christian girl	Unchristian girl #1	Unchristian girl #2
bold about her faith	sympathetic toward Christians	antagonistic
defensive about her faith	defensive about her personal sins	militantly atheistic
apologetic about her faith	interested in Christ	promoting a godless cult
antagonistic toward unbelievers	doesn't believe in the Bible	thinks churches are full of hypocrites

Getting Started

Sample teacher instructions for using in-basket in a Bible Exploration activity:

"We've been discussing what the Bible has to say about sharing our faith, and we have explored some methods that teens can employ in sharing their faith with their unchristian friends. Now we're going to create some true-to-life situations in which we can practice some of these principles. May I have three girls volunteer for a roleplay situation? Thank you Gayle, Lisa and Laurie. Gayle, you are playing the role of a Christian girl who is interested in sharing her faith in Christ. Lisa and Laurie, you are both unchristian girls who are sitting with Gayle over a Coke trying to find out why she spends so much time at church rather than with you in some of your less-than-Christian activities. As you are carrying on your conversation, you will be handed slips of paper from time to time giving you a different slant on your role to play. As you receive your new assignments, try to work them into the character you are representing, while at the same time responding to the changes in the other two characters. Remember, in the midst of your changing roles think about the principles we have already talked about and let them influence your actions."

Sharing Bible Learning

"You three did a marvelous job of keeping up with the different assignments which kept dropping into your 'in-basket.' Now let's discuss what you did, how you felt about it and how we as observers felt about what we saw. Let's begin by having each of you tell which in-basket role you were most comfortable with and uncomfortable with. How hard was it for you, Gayle, to follow the principles for witnessing we talked about with your changing roles and the changing roles of your friends? What observations do some of you viewing learners have as to what went on during the roleplay?"

INTERVIEW

Purpose: That learners
● relate the details of a Bible event and/or the feelings and insights of a Bible character through the medium of an imaginary interview of one or more Bible characters.
● interview present-day people concerning topics being studied.

Materials
☐ Bible for each learner
☐ Interview props such as simulated microphone, TV camera, costumes, etc. (optional)

Procedure
1. Learners read pre-selected Bible narrative, noting the key events and characters.
2. Groups of learners work together preparing an imaginary interview of one or more of the principal characters by one or more interviewers.
3. Learners present their interview to the class and discuss the concepts presented.

Variations
1. Learners may record their interviews on audio or video cassette for presentation as a simulated radio or TV interview.
2. Interviews may be used in a contemporary setting as learners apply Bible principles to life situations (see Example B).

Examples
   Example A: The following partial script was designed to relate the details of Jesus driving the merchants from the Temple as recorded in John 2:13-16.
   John: This is the apostle John speaking to you live on station KJON from the scene of one of the most bizarre events in the history of the Temple. I'm gathering information so that this event may be included in my soon-to-be-released Gospel According to Saint John. I'm going to be talking with several people who were eyewitnesses to the event. Sir, you were here during the happening, weren't you?
   Animal merchant: Here?! Yes, I was here—right in the middle of it!
   John: Could you tell our listeners what happened?
   Animal merchant: I was sitting at my booth here in the courtyard of the Temple, selling the sacrificial animals as I have each year. There were several of us selling animals—and it was very busy since we were running a two-for-one sale on sheep. All of a sudden this so-called rabbi who thinks He is some kind of Temple strong man marches into the Temple. Before you could say Mephibosheth he picked up a whip and started driving all the animals out of the courtyard.
   John: What did you do?
   Animal merchant: What *could* I do? He had a whip and fire in his eyes. I ran for cover.
   John: Sir, you were there too, weren't you? What was your impression of the incident?
   Money changer: Yes, I was there. I was working in the money-changing booth, a

70

service to our brothers who come from out of the country with foreign currency. And in the midst of our good deed—for which we charged a mere 50 percent fee—this wild man comes in and knocks over our tables, sending coins crashing across the cobblestones. We are ruined! The beggars scooped up the money and ran before we could retrieve even half of it.

John: Did this rabbi give any explanation for what he did?

Money changer: He kept shouting at us, "How dare you turn my Father's house into a market!" He's going to pay for this.

John: Ladies and gentlemen, here He is—the rabbi named Jesus who turned the Temple court upside down today. Jesus, could you talk with us for a moment?

Example B: The following interview script is one group's way of relating various opinions teens have today of Jesus Christ.

Newsman: This is your man-on-the-street interviewer here on the corner of First and Main, taking an opinion poll from those passing by. Today's question is: What do you think of Jesus Christ? You sir, would you give us your response to the question?

Man #1: Jesus Christ? A name out of the past that has no relevance to modern times. Good for my grandmother maybe, but not for me.

Newsman: And you, ma'm, what do you think of Jesus Christ?

Woman #1: A great teacher, a wonderful influence on mankind, but I don't know about this stuff saying He is the Son of God.

Newsman: And you, sir?

Getting Started

Sample teacher instructions for using the interview in a Bible Exploration activity:

"Turn to John 2:13-16 with me. As I read, would you follow along in your Bibles and let your imagination relive the verses I'm going to read. Try to see the people involved and try to visualize all the action. 'When it was almost time . . .

"Could you see the action happening as I read? Let's climb into a time machine and travel back there to talk to the persons involved. Let's each take the identity of one of the characters involved—an animal merchant, a money changer, a dove seller, Jesus and some of the disciples. Imagine that I am a man-on-the-street interviewer and I want the facts on what happened in this incident. When I interview you, base your responses on what the Bible says and how your imagination fills in the details not mentioned in the passage. Who would like to be the animal merchant?"

Sharing Bible Learning

"Interviewing some of you as I did makes me almost feel like I was there myself. Did you feel that way? Let's talk for a few minutes about what happened in these verses we have dramatized. Why did Jesus drive these people from the Temple?"

PLAY PRESENTATION

Purpose: That learners simulate biblical principles in true-to-life settings through formal dramatization.

Materials
☐ Suitable play and scripts for each participant
☐ Necessary props
☐ Suitable location for presentation

Procedure
1. Learners prepare in advance by rehearsing a play which demonstrates biblical principles of a given lesson.
2. Play participants present the play as a part of the lesson.
3. Observers discuss among themselves and with the participants the principles illustrated in the play.

Variations
1. Learners may write a play for presentation instead of using a published script. An original play must be written and rehearsed in advance of the lesson.
2. Play reading is a simpler form of play presentation, where props and staging are eliminated. Participants rehearse and then read the play in class.
3. Plays may be presented to the class by outside groups—professionals, other age groups, etc.—to stimulate discussion by the class as a whole.

Examples
Following is one idea for the use of play presentation illustrating biblical principles:

One class was studying a unit on witnessing. At the beginning of the unit a small, volunteer drama team was formed to write and present a play summarizing the principles of witnessing which would be discussed during the unit. The drama team met outside of class during the four-week unit—discussing the principles being presented in class, determining a setting in which those principles might be dramatized and writing a script. The team wrote a play dramatizing a Christian young person on trial as an ineffective witness. The cast consisted of the defendant, a prosecuting attorney, a defense attorney, a few witnesses and a judge. During the trial the defense sought to prove that the defendant had been a sufficient witness on the basis of the principles previously discussed in class. The prosecution attempted to prove the defendant an unfit witness. When the play was presented to the rest of the class, the class served as the jury and on the basis of the evidence presented determined the guilt or innocence of the defendant. Discussion followed the play, effectively reviewing and confirming the principles the unit had presented.

Getting Started
Sample teacher instructions for using play presentation in a Bible Exploration activity:

"During this unit we have been talking about principles of witnessing for Christ presented by the Scriptures. As we have discussed the principles, we have been learning how to practice these principles in our life at school and among our other friends. While we have been working on this unit in class, our drama team has worked very hard outside of class to prepare a play which will help us conclude this unit in a special way. Our drama team is going to present an original play during which a Christian teen will be on trial for being an ineffective witness. We will be the jury. At the conclusion of the play, we will discuss the evidence presented and reach a verdict on whether the defendant was guilty or innocent of the charges. As you watch, think of the principles for witnessing we have been discussing."

Sharing Bible Learning

"What a great job our drama team did! I appreciate all the extra work that went into their very stimulating play. Now let's discuss the evidence presented and try to arrive at a verdict based on the principles we have been discussing."

DRAMA ACTIVITIES

ROLEPLAY

Purpose: That learners spontaneously act out given emotions and roles in specific true-to-life situations in order to emphasize lesson goals.

Materials
☐ Clearly defined written roleplay assignments
☐ Necessary props

Procedure
1. Learners are presented with a biblical or life-related problem situation and specific roles and/or feelings within the situation to be acted out.
2. Assigned players study briefly their assigned roles in preparation for spontaneous drama.
3. Participants play their roles for one to five minutes or until the teacher feels the goals of the roleplay have been met.
4. Observers and participants discuss the roleplay in light of the lesson goals.

Variations
1. A roleplay may be repeated after discussion, changing the roles or emotions to be played by the main characters.
2. "In-basket" assignments may be suggested during the course of the roleplay in order to alter the setting (see "In-basket" on page 68).
3. Roleplays may be done as pantomime, making participants express their roles through actions rather than words.

Example
The following roleplay assignments were given to help learners explore the feelings the prodigal son, his elder brother and his father held for each other after the prodigal had returned.

It is the day following the welcome home feast for the prodigal son. You are playing the role of the **prodigal** and you are grateful to your father for restoration to the family and eager to build a new, loving relationship with your brother.

It is the day following the welcome home feast for the prodigal son. You are playing the role of the **father** and you are hopeful that your wandering son will become more responsible and anxious that your elder son will be accepting of his younger brother.

It is the day following the welcome home feast for the prodigal son. You are playing the role of the **elder son** and you are angry at your father for his generosity to your younger brother, and you are bitterly resentful toward your brother because of what he got away with.

Getting Started

Sample teacher instructions for using roleplay in a Bible Exploration activity:

"What an interesting story—a wayward son being welcomed home by his father after wasting his life and wealth in a wild, fruitless fling. How do you suppose the three principal characters felt after it was all over? What might have been on their minds? Let's have three volunteers who will help us get a better idea of what a meeting between these three might have been like on the day after the feast, and how each might have been feeling toward the others. Larry, Chet and Chuck you seem to be eager to participate in this roleplay. We have already read the story—here are your written assignments. Study them quietly for the next two minutes while we rearrange the room and create an area for you to work in. Plan to give two-three minutes of spontaneous conversation depicting the roles you are assigned . . .

"Those of you who will be observing the roleplays be alert to note the attitudes and feelings each character is expressing so we may discuss them at the conclusion of the activity."

Sharing Bible Learning

"Men, you did a great job of helping us see how these three characters from the Bible story might have felt and acted after the event was all over. Let's talk about what we saw. Who could describe the attitude which the prodigal son was expressing during the conversation? How was he feeling about his father and his brother? . . .

"Good discussion! Many of you contributed some helpful insights into the behavior of the Bible characters. Let's tackle one more question: How might have the behavior of each character been different if each was conducting himself with the attitude of a mature Christian? . . ."

DRAMA ACTIVITIES

SKIT

Purpose: That learners illustrate biblical principles in a true-to-life situation through brief, informal dramatization.

Materials
☐ Written skit assignments
☐ Necessary props

Procedure
1. Learners study pre-selected passages of Scripture, looking for principles suggested by lesson theme.
2. Groups of learners prepare informal, brief skits which illustrate the biblical principles in a contemporary setting.
3. Learners present skits and discuss the principles in light of the skit's contemporary setting.

Variations
1. Two skits may be presented on the same theme—one illustrating the correct application of the biblical principle and the other showing an incorrect application or avoidance of the principle.
2. Different groups may present skits to the large group, with the large group guessing the principle which each skit group is illustrating.

Examples
One class studied five qualities of love as expressed in 1 Corinthians 13:4: "Love is patient, love is kind. It does not envy, it does not boast, it is not proud." The class was divided into five groups and each group was assigned one of the qualities from 1 Corinthians 13:4 to illustrate in a skit showing that quality of love toward a school friend. Group one showed a girl exercising patience toward her locker partner who kept avoiding her responsibility to clean up the locker. Group two illustrated the kindness of love by showing a Christian boy befriending a handicapped schoolmate who had been ridiculed by other students. Group three contrasted the response of two girls trying out for cheerleader upon learning that a third girl had been chosen: one acting and speaking enviously while the other was truly happy for the winner and not personally envious. Group four showed four students discussing their recent mid-term grades with a Christian modestly expressing thanks to God for his good grades while the others boasted in their success. Group five showed the humility of a club president, eager to show his love for God and his fellow students, staying late after a club function to assist the clean-up committee chairman when his committee failed to show up.

Getting Started
Sample teacher instructions for using skits in a Bible Exploration activity:
"We've been discussing several qualities of love today as they are given to us in 1 Corinthians 13:4. As we have talked together I think we have come up with some very helpful definitions for each of the five qualities found in this verse. Now it's

time to see if we can illustrate these qualities in a setting that is familiar to us—our school life. You've been arranged into five groups, and I'm assigning each group one of the qualities of love found in today's verse. Notice that your written assignment requests you to prepare a skit illustrating how your assigned quality would look in the life of a Christian student who was determined to show Christlike love in his school. You have five minutes to prepare your skits. Then we will present them to one another and discuss how we can show love in the school setting."

Sharing Bible Learning

"I visited each one of the groups while you worked, and I'm impressed with the effort you put into your skits. I'm sure we will all have a better understanding of how to apply our Christian love in the school setting after we view and discuss these skits. Group one, will you present your skit for us please?

"Thank you for that excellent presentation! Let's all talk about it before we go on to group two. What was the basic quality of love that group one was presenting? How did they show that quality within the school setting? What are some other ways to show patience when we are at school?

"Alright, group two, we're ready to see what you have done."

DRAMA ACTIVITIES

TV/RADIO SHOW

Purpose: That learners express insights gained in Bible study through the format of a mock radio or TV program.

Materials
☐ Written program script
☐ Necessary props (including dummy microphones, sets, etc.)

Procedure
1. Learners read pre-selected passages of Scripture looking for main ideas.
2. Groups of learners prepare a mock radio or TV program as a vehicle for sharing their insights with the other learners.
3. Groups present their "programs" for each other and discuss their insights together.

Variations
1. Where facilities allow, mock radio programs may be recorded on audio cassettes, and TV programs recorded on video cassettes, for presentation to the class.
2. Radio or TV programs may be presented to other departments.
3. Formats of specific popular programs may be adapted to fit the purpose of the presentation.

Examples
The following are several possible radio/TV formats for sharing Bible information and insights:

A news program format would be excellent for presenting the account of the stoning of Stephen in Acts 7. An anchorman could host the program from the studio in Jerusalem and "on-the-spot" interviewers could talk with witnesses.

A game show format may be used to review the facts of Paul's missionary journeys. A contemporary television game show would provide the setting for contestants to be asked questions by the host, be awarded prizes for successful answers and even select a champion in the category.

A dramatic format might be best to present a narrative which is charged with emotion, such as Joseph's reunion with his brothers in Egypt.

Commercials can be utilized to "sell" biblical principles or qualities such as faith, wisdom, forbearance or encouragement. Commercials could also be used to give class announcements.

Getting Started
Sample instructions for using a TV show format in a Bible Exploration activity:
"In order to explore some of the details and feelings surrounding the death of

Stephen in Acts 7, we are going to approach the event as a television news team might have if there had been television in those days. We're going to produce a mock television news program covering all sides of the story. Group one, would you serve as the studio newscasters? You will give the facts of the story as they are found in Acts 7. Group two, will you prepare an interview of several of the people who killed Stephen, trying to find out why they did so and what they were feeling as Stephen preached? Group three, we also need to interview several of Stephen's Christian brothers and sisters, some of whom watched him die. Try to gather some insight into what might have been going on in them as they stood by helplessly during the ordeal. We need one person from the studio team to serve as the anchorman and introduce each commentator and interviewer. Thank you, Jeff—you will be a great anchorman! You have ten minutes to put together your part of the program. Jeff will be visiting each group as he puts the program together."

Sharing Bible Learning

"I see that our three news teams are 'on location' for their reports. Jeff, our anchorman, is at his desk. If everyone is ready, we are on the air with the news.

"Thank you for that thorough examination of the Bible account of Stephen's death. You identified the facts, brought to light some of the issues behind the event and gave us a good inside look at what some of the people present might have been thinking and saying. You really made the Bible come alive today! Now let's talk about what we have done. What personal insights did you receive as you prepared your news program? What did you notice about this seemingly tragic event that you had not noticed until you started to dig up some details to report?"

Jr. High   Sr. High

ADD A VERSE

Purpose: That learners express their response to a Bible theme or principle by writing a new verse to a hymn, with words about that theme.

Materials
☐ Hymnbooks or a copy of the hymn for each learner
☐ Chart with blanks for each syllable or note in the song to be used
☐ Writing paper
☐ Pens or pencils
☐ Musical accompaniment (optional)

Procedure
1. Learners discuss the lesson theme or principle and identify main ideas.
2. Individuals or groups working together write a new verse to a familiar hymn, expressing the lesson theme in their own words. They fill in the blanks on the prepared chart (see "Materials" above).
3. Learners sing their new verses to each other or with each other and discuss the words in light of the lesson theme.

Variations
1. New verses can be written on poster paper or overhead transparencies for classroom display.
2. New verses can be written by a group expressing an application of a Bible principle, or by individuals expressing personal responses to a Bible principle.
3. New verses can be written to contemporary gospel songs or secular songs as well as hymns.

Examples
The following verse—to the tune of "Trust and Obey"—was written by a group studying the book of Job and discussing the theme of trusting God in the midst of afflictions and problems. Their verse was an application of the biblical principle of trust in God to the problems encountered in school.

When I worry in class, wond'ring if I will pass,
When I'm doing the best that I can;
I continue to pray, ask God's help every day
And give thanks that I'm part of His plan.
"Trust Him in school," is my day-by-day rule.
I give Jesus my problems, and I trust Him in school.

Getting Started
Sample teacher instructions for using "add a verse" in a Bible Exploration activity:

"We all agree that Job had a pretty rough experience and that none of us would want to trade places with him. But let's face it—we have troubles too! Maybe not to the degree that Job had troubles, but we do have our share. I think one of the reasons God gave us Job's story in the Bible is so that we might have some help in knowing how to handle our troubles when they come. What are some areas of our life as teenagers where we can run into trouble? School? Relating to parents? Relationships among friends? All of these qualify as 'trouble spots' from time to time. A very familiar hymn gives us some good suggestions on trusting God in the midst of trouble. Let's sing a verse of the hymn together, and then we are going to do something very unique with this hymn tune. Rhonda, can you give us a starting chord on the guitar?

"I would like each group to select one of the areas that we identified as possible 'trouble spots' in our lives. I'll give you 30 seconds to decide which area you are going to work on.

"I would like each group to write a new verse to the hymn we have just sung, 'Trust and Obey,' which conveys the principle of trusting God in the area of trouble you have just selected. You will have eight minutes to write your verse—if you finish early, you may write a new chorus to go along with your new verse. Letter your completed verse on a sheet of poster paper."

Sharing Bible Learning

"Thank you for the creative and thoughtful energy you have put into your verse writing project. Let's post the verses around the room and have each group sing their verse for us one time. Then we will all sing the entire set of new verses together.

"Great singing! Now let's summarize the principles we have been singing about—trusting God in trouble. I will list them on the chalkboard as you speak them out. What have we learned about trust today?"

COMMERCIAL JINGLE

Purpose: That learners summarize a scriptural principle by creating and singing a simple, catchy jingle.

Materials
☐ Writing paper
☐ Pens and pencils
☐ Musical accompaniment (optional)

Procedure
1. Learners read pre-selected passage of Scripture, looking for main ideas relating to lesson theme.
2. Learners summarize their discoveries and write them in the form of a commercial jingle, using the familiar tune of a current radio or TV commercial.
3. Learners share their jingles with each other and discuss them in light of the lesson theme.

Variations
Commercial jingles may be used in conjunction with visual advertisement (posters, billboards, etc.) or dramatized presentations (skits, TV programs, etc.).

Examples
When selecting a jingle tune to use . . .

LOOK FOR	AVOID
Simple tunes	Difficult tunes
Familiar tunes	Obscure tunes
Tunes reflecting wholesome advertising	Tunes advertising questionable products

The following themes lend themselves more readily to commercial jingles:
1. Passages which "sell" qualities which are to be desired in the Christian life (i.e. faith, wisdom, love, patience, etc.).
2. Passages in which messages are being exchanged between Bible characters (i.e. Barnabas commending Saul to the Jerusalem church [Acts 9:26,27], Moses and Aaron speaking to Pharaoh [Ex. 5:1]).

Getting Started
Sample teacher instructions for using a commercial jingle in a Bible Exploration activity:

"Our study of the New Testament character Barnabas has brought us to Acts 9 and his first involvement with Saul. As we have looked at Barnabas in other portions of Scripture we have seen that he had qualities of encouragement among people which greatly affected the relationships of the people around him. Acts 9:26,27 are no exception. Imagine that you are Barnabas coming to speak to the disciples at Jerusalem regarding the recently converted Saul. You know that the disciples are suspicious of Saul, since he was so recently involved in arresting and imprisoning Christians. Being a man of encouragement, you want to introduce Saul to the disciples in a special way—by singing a commercial jingle which will recommend this new believer to the disciples. You are to create a commercial jingle to the tune of the commercial for the city bank—you've all heard that tune on the radio, haven't you? In your commercial jingle, you are trying to "sell" Saul to the disciples by including in your song as many positive qualities about him as you can get in. You have 10 minutes to put together your jingle."

Sharing Bible Learning

"I appreciate the enthusiasm I have seen as you have worked on your jingles. I can't wait to hear the completed products. Who will be the first to share their jingle with us?

"Now let's review the qualities of Paul which you have summarized in your jingles. You call them out, and I'll list them."

GROUP SINGING

Purpose: That learners express Bible principles and their applications of Bible principles to life through the medium of music.

Materials
☐ Hymn books, song books or song sheets
☐ Musical accompaniment (optional)

Procedure
1. Learners explore Scripture passages relating to the lesson theme and discuss application of these principles to their lives.
2. In the course of their study, learners are led in singing hymns, songs or choruses which parallel the lesson theme and assist in communicating the principles involved.

Variations
1. Recorded music may be used as background for, or in place of, live group singing. Recorded selections should be chosen on the basis of their relevancy to the lesson theme.
2. Group singing may precede, accompany and/or follow the Bible study, being used wherever appropriate to accomplish the lesson goals.
3. In some instances, specially prepared music—solos, duets, ensembles, etc.— may accompany or replace group singing in class.

Examples
The following are several suggestions for using group singing in a variety of ways in the course of a standard lesson plan focusing on the theme of God's faithfulness:

Approach: Introducing the theme of faithfulness
Group Singing: One or two songs stating the faithfulness of God
Bible Exploration: Exploring and applying Bible principles relating God's faithfulness to His people
Conclusion and Decision: Individuals thank God for His faithfulness to them in a specific area

Approach: Introducing the theme of faithfulness
Bible Exploration: Exploring and applying Bible principles relating God's faithfulness to His people
Group Singing: One or two songs thanking God for His faithfulness
Conclusion and Decision: Individuals thank God for His faithfulness to them in a specific area

Group Singing: One or two songs stating the faithfulness of God
Approach: Introducing the theme of faithfulness
Bible Exploration: Exploring and applying Bible principles relating God's

faithfulness to His people

> **Solo:** One song thanking God for His faithfulness
>
> **Conclusion and Decision:** Individuals thank God for His faithfulness to them in a specific area

Getting Started

Sample teacher instructions for using group singing in a Conclusion and Decision activity:

"Even though we may not totally understand it, we see from our Scripture study today that God is faithful to His people, even when we are not completely faithful to Him. We have identified some areas in our lives where we are recognizing His faithfulness. And in just a moment we will express to God personally our response to His faithfulness. But right now, let's sing together the chorus of a familiar hymn which states, 'Great is Thy faithfulness.' Let's concentrate on singing these words to Him as a group response to His faithfulness to us. The words are on your song sheet; let's sing together. 'Great is Thy faithfulness, Great is Thy faithfulness, Morning by morning new mercies I see.'"

Sharing Bible Learning

"One of the lines of the chorus we have just sung states, "All I have needed Thy hand hath provided.' Can you think of one thing you have 'needed' this past week which God has faithfully 'provided' for you? It may be something common to all of us, or it may be something quite unique that God has provided for you this week. Would you write down on your worksheet a couple of sentences of thanks to God for His faithfulness in providing something you needed this week."

Jr. High   Sr. High

HYMN/SONG RESPONSE

Purpose: That learners express their understanding and response to Bible principles which are related in hymns or Christian songs.

Materials
☐ Hymnbooks, songbooks or song sheets
☐ Writing paper
☐ Pens or pencils
☐ Hymn/song response questions for each learner (photocopied or mimeographed)

Procedure
1. Learners are directed to Bible passages and asked to look for main ideas relating to lesson theme.
2. Learners are given copies of a hymn or Christian song which relates to the lesson theme. (Be sure to observe copyright restrictions on copying material.)
3. Learners write and/or discuss response to the hymn or song based on specific questions or instructions from the teacher.

Variations
1. Hymns or songs—and response questions—may be written on poster paper, overhead transparencies or chalkboard for classroom display.
2. Recorded music may be used to present the hymns or songs in addition to written text.
3. Individuals or groups of learners may compose their response as another verse to the hymn or song they are studying.

Examples
The following hymn/song response exercise was used following a study of Philippians 2:5-11, focusing on the ultimate Lordship of Jesus Christ. The hymn "Jesus Shall Reign" was introduced and the following questions were presented to learners for response from the hymn:
1. Where does the hymn suggest that Jesus' lordship will prevail?
2. How long does the hymn indicate Jesus' lordship over the earth will last?
3. What does the hymn suggest will be the response of people to the lordship of Christ on the earth?
4. What kind of people does the hymn state are involved in a positive response to Jesus' lordship?
5. Can you think of additional Scripture verses which validate each of the hymn's statements on the first four questions?

Getting Started
Sample teacher instructions for using hymn/song response in a Bible Exploration activity:
"As you have mentioned, Philippians 2:5-11 gives us a picture of the ultimate lordship of Jesus Christ before whom, 'every knee should bow . . . and every

tongue confess.' Another expression of that same thought is found in a hymn titled, 'Jesus Shall Reign.' On your worksheet you have five questions which will lead you to take a closer look at the hymn in light of our discussion of Philippians 2:5-11. Work together in groups of four answering the questions. Notice that the hymn lyrics are reproduced for you on the worksheet. You have about seven minutes to complete the assignment."

Sharing Bible Learning

"Thank you for getting into the discussion so thoroughly. I was pleased to see most all of you offering your valuable insights on this subject of the lordship of Jesus Christ. Let's compare notes with one another by sharing our answers to the questions on the worksheet. Group three, what were some of the things you talked about in response to question 1, 'Where does the hymn suggest that Jesus' lordship will prevail?'? Yes, the hymn states he will reign wherever the sun goes. Is there any place on earth where the sun does not shine at least sometime? No! Then where shall Jesus' reign be found? Right! Everywhere!"

JESUS SHALL REIGN

Isaac Watts   John Hatton

WORDS: ISAAC WATTS (FROM PSALM 72). MUSIC: JOHN HATTON.
ARRANGEMENT © COPYRIGHT 1966 BY GOSPEL LIGHT PUBLICATIONS. USED BY PERMISSION.

Jr. High   Sr. High

HYMN/SONG WRITING

Purpose: That learners participate in creating an original hymn or song which reflects the Scriptural principles of the lesson or unit studied.

Materials
☐ Writing paper
☐ Pens and pencils
☐ Musical accompaniment

Procedure
1. Learners read pre-selected passage of Scripture, looking for main ideas relating to lesson theme.
2. Learners summarize their discoveries and use their summaries to compose lyrics which capture the essence of the Scripture passage. Lyrics may be written to a familiar tune (hymn, Christian song, secular song, etc.).
3. Learners share their original composition with other classes or the entire congregation.

NOTE: This activity requires at least one musically-gifted individual who can compose an original tune.

Variations
1. Learners may compose the song over two or more weeks of a unit of study, completing the song on the final meeting. Outside-of-class work may also be done on the song.
2. Key Scripture verses may be set to music to aid in memorization.
3. Compose an original tune and lyrics which capture the essence of a Scripture passage.

Examples
The following themes lend themselves more readily to original songwriting:
1. Lists of qualities such as the beatitudes (Matt. 5:3-12), the fruit of the Spirit (Gal. 5:22,23), "Think about such things" (Phil. 4:8), etc.
2. Descriptions such as faith (Heb. 11:1,6), love (1 Cor. 13:4-8), wisdom (James 3:13-18), etc.
3. Commands such as Ephesians 5:19,20; 1 Thessalonians 5:16-22; Romans 12:9-21; etc.

Getting Started
Sample teacher instructions for using hymn/song writing in a Bible Exploration activity:

"We have listed several instructions to believers from Romans 12:9-21—Paul seems to be able to pack so much into so few verses! One way to help these thoughts really stick with us is to put them into the form of a song. You know how easy it is to remember a commercial jingle from the radio or TV. And since each of our groups has at least one person with some music background, I would like each group to compose an original song from a section of our lesson text: group one will work with Romans 12:9-13, group two with Romans 12:14-16, and group three with Romans 12:17-21. We're not trying to create a lavish Broadway musical, but to take the truths found in God's word and set them to a simple tune to help us remember them better. You don't need to follow verbatim the wording in the text, but make sure your lyrics reflect the meaning of each section as we discussed them. You have 20 minutes to work, beginning now."

Sharing Bible Learning

"Let's have each group share their original song with us, and after you sing it, we will try to learn it, too. Carlos, I see your group is ready and you have your guitar in place. Would you begin our sharing time by singing your song?"

Jr. High   Sr. High

BIBLE READING/RECITATION

Purpose: That learners become personally involved in Scripture content through reading or reciting Scripture aloud.

Materials
☐ Bible for each learner
☐ Written Bible reading/recitation assignments

Procedure
1. Before the class session, teacher directs selected learners to familiarize themselves with the Bible passage for the upcoming lesson by making specific study assignments.
2. Learners prepare individually for in-class reading or recitation.
3. Appointed learners read or recite Scripture verses at the appropriate time in the lesson.
4. All learners follow teacher instructions to explore and apply to their own lives the lesson Scripture.

Variations
1. The simplest form of this activity is to have learners read lesson Scriptures aloud in class with no prior preparation. This is best accomplished by asking volunteers to read or by assigning reading tasks only to those learners who would not be threatened by reading a Scripture passage unprepared.
2. Two or more learners may prepare and read/recite the same passage of Scripture from different translations or versions.
3. Learners may prepare and read Bible passages onto cassette tape for presentation in class.
4. Scripture reading or recitation may be presented as a drama (see "Act Out Scripture" on page 66).
5. As appointed learners read or recite aloud, other learners may pantomime the Scripture passage being read.

Example
Sample written Bible reading assignment:

Thank you for agreeing to prepare and read from Psalm 51 during our lesson this coming Sunday. Our lesson theme is, "Confessing Sin, Receiving Forgiveness." Psalm 51 is King David's confession of the sin of adultery with Bathsheba and the murder of her husband. Here is your assignment:
1. In order to get a background for Psalm 51, read 2 Samuel 11 and 12.
2. Read Psalm 51:1-6 several times aloud, practicing pronunciation and becoming acquainted with the phrasing. Try to be so familiar with this passage that you can look up at your audience from time to time while reading.
3. Two other students will be reading Psalm 51:7-12 and 13-19 after you have completed your reading.

4. If you have any questions about pronunciation or phrasing, feel free to give me a call.

Getting Started

Sample teacher instructions for using Bible reading in a Bible Exploration activity:

"One of the key elements in our study of sin is the theme of confession and forgiveness. Today we are going to hear the written confession of a man who was an adulterer and a murderer, and we are going to discuss how God viewed this man. But first, let's get some background information on this man and what he did. He was King David and his story is found in 2 Samuel 11 and 12. Let me recap the highlights.

"David fell to temptation in his affair with Bathsheba, and he compounded his sin by having her husband Uriah killed. But David did the right thing in the face of confrontation with his sin—he confessed it and received forgiveness. Cheryl, Vikki and John are prepared to read David's confession for us this morning. Listen as they read to us what David wrote in Psalm 51 after being confronted with his sin. As you listen, jot down any questions which arise in your mind as they read."

Sharing Bible Learning

"Thank you, Cheryl, Vikki and John, for your excellent reading. What questions did those of you listening have while these three were reading?"

ORAL PRESENTATION

CHORAL READING

Purpose: That learners express personal responses to certain passages of Scripture by writing and reading a response in unison.

Materials
☐ Bible for each learner
☐ Written choral reading script for each learner

Procedure
1. Before the class session, specific groups of learners are assigned verses to study, looking for main ideas.
2. Selected groups compose a written response to their assigned verse(s).
3. Each written response is inserted into the completed script for the choral reading. (Script may be photocopied. Or, it may be written on poster paper taped to the wall, on an overhead transparency or on the chalkboard.)
4. In class, learners who prepared script read it to the other learners.
5. Class members discuss concepts presented in the choral reading.

Variations
1. Choral readings may be formed from one section of Scripture, with composed responses being read in response to succeeding verses or from several related verses from different parts of the Bible.
2. Choral readings may be presented as dramatic readings which can be prepared in class.

Example
The following choral reading script was composed after several groups had studied Psalm 8 and composed written responses which were arranged into script form. The teacher read the verses from Psalm 8 and each group read its response in unison.

Teacher: O Lord, our Lord, how majestic is your name in all the earth! You have set your glory above the heavens.

Group 1: God, your name is spoken in every language with awe and reverence. Even men who deny your existence respond to the intricacy of your handiwork which shines down on us from the heavens above.

Teacher: From the lips of children and infants you have ordained praise because of your enemies, to silence the foe and the avenger.

Group 2: In comparison to your greatness and glory we are mere children. But you have chosen us to be creatures of praise to you from hearts that choose to love you. And even in our simple worship the enemy of our souls is defeated.

Teacher: When I consider your heavens, the work of your fingers, the moon and the stars, which you have set in place, what is man that you are mindful of him, the son of man that you care for him?

Group 3: It boggles our mind, Lord, that in all of creation—the vastness of the universe which is bigger than our comprehension—that you are concerned with sinful individuals like us. We seem so small in comparison to all else you have made. But we do respond to your love, even though we don't completely know why you offer it to us.

Getting Started

Sample teacher instructions for using choral reading in a Bible Exploration activity:

"In anticipation of our study today on God's greatness, three groups have prepared a presentation to help us become familiar with today's Scripture portion and a response to it. I would like the three groups who met this week and prepared their responses to Psalm 8:1-4 to join me in front of class as we present a choral reading based on these verses."

Sharing Bible Learning

"Now let's open our Bibles together to Psalm 8 and discuss some of the thoughts which were illustrated in the choral reading. First of all, what do you think is meant by the use of the word 'Lord' twice in the first four words? In other words, why does the psalm writer say, 'O LORD, our Lord' instead of just saying, 'O LORD'?"

Jr. High   Sr. High

ONE-MINUTE SERMON

Purpose: That learners express individually their response to lesson Scriptures through a brief, impromptu speech.

Materials
☐ Bibles for each learner

Procedure
1. Learners are directed to pre-selected Bible passages.
2. Each learner is asked to prepare a one-minute oral response to one of the verses read (or a section of a verse), commenting on what the verse says or means.
3. Learners share their one-minute sermons with each other.
NOTE: If you have learners who are uncomfortable with this activity, have *volunteers* prepare and present the one-minute sermons.

Variations
1. Write the key lesson verses on index cards. Each learner selects a card, reads the verse and responds immediately with their verbal response for one minute.
2. Assign verses to groups of learners. Each group prepares a one-minute sermon which only one member of the group presents to the class.

Example
The following verses were used for a series of one-minute sermons on the subject of faith. Each verse is followed by a simple outline. Two or three sentences were shared from each point on the outline:

"Now faith is being sure of what we hope for and certain of what we do not see" (Hebrews 11:1).
1. Some Christians think faith is blind and formless.
2. This verse says that faith provides the substance of things we are hoping for in the Lord.
3. Faith helps us see with spiritual eyes what we cannot yet see with physical eyes.

"And without faith it is impossible to please God, because anyone who comes to him must believe that he exists and that he rewards those who earnestly seek him" (Hebrews 11:6).
1. We must exercise faith to please God.
2. We must exercise faith just to come to God.
3. When we come to God in faith he rewards us.

"Faith by itself, if it is not accompanied by action, is dead" (James 2:17).
1. Faith was never intended to stand by itself.
2. Faith was designed to be linked with action.
3. Faith is dead until the action designed to accompany it makes faith alive.

Getting Started
Sample teacher instructions for using one-minute sermons in a Bible Exploration activity:

"The Bible says a lot about faith. And it seems that each Bible verse on faith is worth a sermon. Today we are going to look at several verses on faith and share several very short sermons with one another. I'm going to give each of you a card containing a Bible reference for a verse on faith. You are to do three things with the verse you receive; First, look it up in your Bible and read it over to yourself several times, thinking about the meaning of the verse. You might answer this question to yourself as you read, 'What does this verse teach me about faith?' Second, jot down on your card two or three key thoughts about faith which this verse gives you. These key thoughts will be the outline for a one-minute sermon you will give us on faith, based on your verse. Third, after we have each prepared, we will deliver our mini-sermons—each person having a maximum of one minute to talk about his/her verse, using the notes you write on your card. Does everyone understand the assignment? Then let's get to work. I'll pass out the cards and pencils, and you have three minutes to prepare."

Sharing Bible Learning

"As a class, we have learned a lot about faith in just a very short time. But we need to share what we have learned with each other. Remember, you have only one minute to share your thoughts with us. Let's begin with the person who was reading Hebrews 11:1. Carla, we are ready for your one-minute sermon. (Carla presents one-minute sermon.)"Thank you, Carla. You have given us some nuggets in your mini-sermon. I especially liked the part about 'the substance of things we are hoping for in the Lord.' What are some things that Christians are hoping for that faith helps us get a hold of?"

MONOLOGUE

Purpose: That learners are exposed to a block of information in as little time as possible through direct lecture.

Materials
☐ Necessary visual aids to accompany monologue

Procedure
1. Teacher reduces monologue content to a simple outline.
2. Teacher arranges for visual aids and/or note sheets to accompany verbal presentation.
3. Teacher presents monologue in class.
4. Learners respond to monologue and discuss principles or information presented.

Variations
1. Monologue content can be broken into small sections with opportunity given for response or discussion as the monologue progresses.
2. Some or all of the monologue content can be prerecorded on cassette tape and played for the learners while the teacher illustrates the content on the chalkboard, overhead transparency, flipchart or other visual aid.
3. Learners may present monologues when they are encouraged to make preparation of material and presentation plan.
4. Person giving monologue may assume character of a Bible person and speak as that person would have.

Examples
Since the monologue, lecture or sermon method of teaching requires little involvement from the learners in itself, care must be taken to supplement the monologue with activities which will involve the learners to a greater dimension during the presentation. The following three avenues of involvement will help keep the learners' interest during the monologue:

Look
The effectiveness of the monologue is greatly increased when learners have something to look at which supports the lecture theme. When relating a historical event from the Bible, a map or timeline for learners to see helps identify events in relation to geography and history. When presenting several points on a given subject, a list, diagram or illustration on the chalkboard keeps learners visually involved. A complete description of audio/visual aids is found in the article, "The Sights and Sounds of Learning" on page 15.

Write
A simple worksheet with the bare outline of your monologue, when placed in the learner's hand along with a pen or pencil, will help him/her gain more from the lecture. Even a blank sheet of paper will provoke some learners to jot down a few key thoughts or reproduce diagrams or illustrations you may use. Worksheets

should have plenty of open space so that learners know that they are responsible to fill in the blanks.

Talk

Monologues which exceed twenty minutes in length should be broken up into at least two smaller sections with time given in between for learners to respond verbally to what has been said. You may ask listeners to "nudge their neighbor" (talk to the person sitting next to them) for one minute, answering one question you have posed from the monologue content. You may call for spontaneous group feedback—"Does anyone have a question or comment about what I have said so far?" Or, you may have several people prearranged to involve a small cluster of people near them in conversation on your monologue theme.

Getting Started

Sample teacher instructions for using monologue in a Bible Exploration activity:

"Today we are beginning our study of the book of Exodus, which finds the people of God, the Israelites, in slavery in Egypt. But how did God's people, who were given the land of Canaan for their own land, end up in Egypt? I want to backtrack with you for a couple of hundred years to answer that question. I will be referring to this map of the general Palestine area and the timeline on the chalkboard with the names of these four major characters—Abraham, Isaac, Jacob and Joseph. You have the same timeline reproduced on your worksheet. I invite you to jot down the key thoughts which help us know how Israel got stuck in Egypt. It all started with Abraham, a man whom God called out of his homeland to establish a nation that God would use to bless the earth."

Sharing Bible Learning

"Before we open our Bibles to Exodus, let's review the key thoughts of what I have just presented to you. What was Abraham called to do?"

PANEL

Purpose: That learners receive information, as a small group with specific knowledge discusses an assigned topic before a class.

Materials
☐ Chairs and table (optional) for the panel members
☐ Assignments for panel preparation

Procedure
1. Teacher selects three or four learners prior to the session to serve as the panel. Teacher informs the panel of their responsibilities and makes specific assignments for their preparation.
2. Panel members research their subject matter before the session.
3. During the class session, teacher poses subject-related questions to the panel and panel members respond based on their research.
4. Class members are invited to ask additional questions of the panel members.

Variations
1. On occasion a panel of "experts" may be invited into the class, having made the same preparation required of any panel. Guest panels may include the pastor, church leaders, parents or outside guests who are qualified to contribute in a given area.

Example
A panel was selected to discuss the implications of various abuses of the physical body in light of 1 Corinthians 6:19,20: "Do you not know that your body is a temple of the Holy Spirit, who is in you, whom you have received from God? You are not your own; you were bought at a price. Therefore honor God with your body."

The panel was asked to research the following questions and come prepared to answer any or all of them before the class:
1. What are the effects of drug abuse on the human body—including "over the counter" drugs, marijuana and "hard" narcotics?
2. What are the effects of tobacco-smoking on the human body—in those who smoke directly and in those who are affected by smokers in the environment?
3. What are the effects of alcohol abuse on the human body—from "social" drinking to alcoholism?
4. What are the effects of overeating on the human body?
5. What are the pros and cons of physical fitness in their relation to health?
6. What do Israel's dietary laws have to do with Paul's command in 1 Corinthians 6:19,20?

Getting Started
Sample teacher instructions for using a panel in a Bible Exploration activity:
"Last week we began a discussion based on 1 Corinthians 6:19,20, and we agreed that, although Paul was writing primarily about illicit sexual activity, the

principles discussed in the verse apply broadly to how we care for our bodies. In preparation for today's session, a panel has been doing some research on present-day abuses of the human body which are more or less accepted in today's culture. I would like the panel to respond to a few questions on the subject. As they do, the rest of the class should jot down any questions which come to mind so that you may address the panel also. First question: What does current information tell us are the effects of drug abuse on the human body, including 'over the counter' drugs, marijuana and 'hard' narcotics? Robin, you have your hand up to reply."

Sharing Bible Learning

"I want to thank the panel for their excellent research—you have provided some good information for our discussion. And I appreciate how you class members have participated in the discussion by adding your questions and comments. I have one more question for all of us and I would like each of you to write your personal response on your worksheet: 'If I were convinced of the importance of taking care of my body as an act of honoring God, what would I need to do differently?' You have two minutes to quietly think and write.

"I wonder if any of you would volunteer to read what you wrote in response to my last question?"

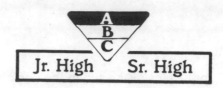

ACROSTIC PUZZLE

Purpose: That learners identify a lesson theme from specific clues given in words or phrases.

Materials
☐ Poster paper, butcher paper or writing paper
☐ Felt markers, pens or pencils
☐ Chalkboard and chalk

Procedure
1. Teacher letters clue words and/or phrases horizontally on large sheet of paper or chalkboard.
2. Learners seek to identify one key word for each clue word or phrase, and write the key word on the paper or chalkboard.
3. When each key word is appropriately written, the first letters of each, read vertically, will spell the lesson theme.

Variations
1. Individual acrostic puzzles can be prepared for duplication on photocopier or mimeograph so each learner may complete the puzzle individually.
2. Simple acrostics will give the learners the opportunity to supply the key phrases for the theme word already lettered on the paper or chalkboard (see "Acrostic" on page 34).
3. Acrostic puzzles can be arranged using Scripture verses or phrases to lead learners to the theme word (see example B).

Examples
Example A: An acrostic puzzle ready to be solved (left) and the same puzzle completed (right).

__ __ __ __	(a present)
__ __ __ __	(not fake)
__ __ __ __ __ __	(how long God's love lasts)
__ __ __ __ __ __	(the greatest gift)
__ __ __ __ __ __ __ __	(to whom is God's love offered)

G i f t	(a present)
R e a l	(not fake)
A l w a y s	(how long God's love lasts)
C h r i s t	(the greatest gift)
E v e r y o n e	(to whom is God's love offered)

Example B: A Scripture verse acrostic puzzle ready to be solved (top box) and the same puzzle completed (bottom box).

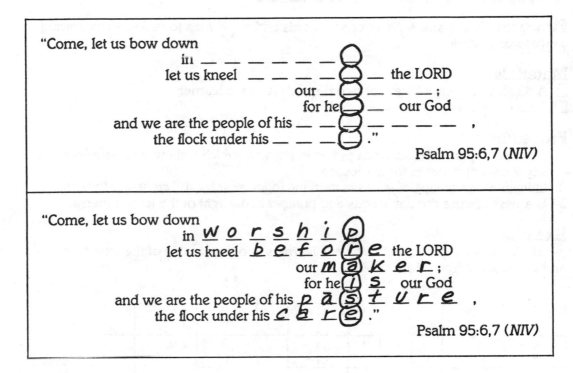

Getting Started

Sample teacher instructions for using an acrostic puzzle in an Approach activity:

"On the chalkboard you will see a brain-teasing puzzle which will start our lesson off today. Notice the spaces down the left-hand column. When the correct letters fill those spaces, the word you find there will be a key word for our Bible study today. To find out which letters fill those spaces, try to figure out the five clue words from the clues given in parentheses. When you have guessed all five clue words correctly, the first letters of those clue words will give you the theme for today. Work together in pairs on your own worksheet beginning now. When you think you have solved the puzzle, signal to me and I will check your work. Let's see which pair can solve the puzzle first."

Sharing Bible Learning

"Sharon and Julianne were the first to solve the puzzle, but many of you were only a few seconds behind them. Let's fill in all the blanks on the chalkboard together. Call them out as I write them in. First, what is a four-letter word for 'a present'? Thank you Kate—'gift' is correct. Now, a four-letter word for 'not fake' (etc.).

"Our key word for today's lesson is what? 'Grace' is correct.

"Why might the word 'gift' be an appropriate clue word for grace? Yes, Sharon, grace *is* a gift—we can't earn it. Why is 'real' a good clue word?"

CROSSWORD PUZZLE

Purpose: That learners discover key words and/or phrases for a lesson by solving a crossword puzzle.

Materials
☐ A duplicated copy of the crossword puzzle for each learner
☐ Pens or pencils

Procedure
1. Teacher prepares a crossword puzzle in advance which will involve learners in key words or phrases for the lesson.
2. Individuals or groups of learners working together solve the crossword puzzle.
3. Learners discuss the key words and phrases in the light of the lesson theme.

Example
The crossword puzzle below* leads learners into the parable of the four soils and its meaning from Mark 4:1-34.

ACROSS

3. Jesus taught many things in _____ (v. 2)
7. _____ of the world can crowd out the Word in a person's life (v. 19)
8. Only he who has ears can do this (vv. 9,23)
9. The Kingdom of God is compared to this small seed (2 words—v.31)
13. Affliction can be withstood only by those with firm _____ in the Word (vv. 16,17)
14. Plants that grew among these were eventually choked out (v. 7)
16. Jesus used many parables to picture or represent the _____ of God (v. 30)
17. The seeds grow _____ and night, but we don't know how (v. 27)
18. In the parables, the seeds are a word picture for the _____ of God (v. 14)

DOWN

1. The deceitfulness of _____ can choke the Word in a person's life (v. 19)
2. The first parable talks about _____ kinds of soil.
3. People not firmly rooted in God may fall away when _____ comes (v. 17)
4. A commonly-used preposition
5. These found shade and nesting space in the branches of the mustard plant (v. 32)
6. He who goes out to sow (plant) (v. 3)
10. He snatches God's Word away from unreceptive hearts as soon as it's planted (v. 32)
11. The seeds that fell in _____ soil grew and produced a harvest (v. 8)
12. The seeds that fell in _____ soil did not have enough soil to become firmly rooted (vv. 5,6)
15. What the mustard seed was eventually able to provide for the birds (v. 32)

Variations

1. One large crossword puzzle may be produced on a large sheet of poster paper or on the chalkboard so the entire class may work on solving it together.
2. Crossword listing is another method using the crossword format for recording Bible discoveries (see "Crossword Listing" on page 38).
3. Learners may create crossword puzzles for each other to solve.

Getting Started

Sample teacher instructions for using crossword puzzle in a Bible Exploration activity:

"We have come to chapter 4 in our Bible study of the Gospel of Mark. The section we are looking at today is 34 verses long, so we are going to use a crossword puzzle to help us get right to the heart of today's theme of growth. On your worksheet you will find a crossword puzzle with Scripture references from Mark 4:1-34 to help you fill in the blanks. Work with a partner for the next 10 minutes solving the puzzle. Then we will talk about what you have found."

Sharing Bible Learning

"Our time is up for solving the puzzle. Even if you are not quite finished, let's bring our attention together and talk through the main ideas of the lesson as we found them in the puzzle. Let's start with number 3 across: 'Jesus taught many things in'—what did you get for that one, Richie? 'Parables' is correct. What is a parable? Why did Jesus teach in parables? Now let's go on to number 7 across."

SCRAMBLED VERSES

Purpose: That learners identify a Bible verse which supports the lesson theme by arranging the words of the verse in correct order.

Materials
☐ A copy of the scrambled verse for each learner (photocopied or mimeographed)
☐ Pens and pencils

Procedure
1. Teacher scrambles the order of the words in a key verse and writes the verse in scrambled order on a sheet of paper for duplication.
2. Individuals or groups of learners working together arrange the verse in correct order.
3. Learners use the unscrambled verse as a discussion-starter for studying the lesson theme.

Variations
1. The scrambled verse may be written on a large sheet of paper. The verse may be cut apart so that each word is on a separate slip of paper. Individuals may work at unscrambling the verse by spreading out the slips of paper on the floor, table or chair and rearranging the words until they discover the correct order.
2. Each word of the scrambled verse may be lettered on a small sheet of poster paper and posted to the wall or a bulletin board. Learners then unscramble the verse by placing the poster sheets in correct order.
3. Key statements supporting the lesson theme may also be scrambled for learners to unscramble.

Examples
The following examples illustrate a scrambled and unscrambled verse (John 16:13a, *NIV*) and a scrambled and unscrambled statement. Notice that capitalization and punctuation are retained in order to give clues to the correct order.

Scrambled

truth,	truth."	of	when	you	he	he,	guide

"But	the	into	all	Spirit	will	comes,

Unscrambled

"But	when	he,	the	Spirit	of	truth,	comes,

he	will	guide	you	into	all	truth."

Scrambled

and	forever.	The	man	to	chief	of	to

end	glorify	is	Him	God	enjoy

Unscrambled

The	chief	end	of	man	is	to	glorify

God	and	to	enjoy	Him	forever.

Getting Started

Sample teacher instructions for using a scrambled verse in an Approach activity:

"Good morning! You will notice that there are three envelopes sitting on the tables around the room. In each envelope is an identical set of words written on slips of paper. The words, when correctly arranged, form a key verse for today's lesson. Let's have the sophomores work together at this table, the juniors at that table and the seniors at the table by the door. Your challenge is to see which group can arrange the verse into its correct order first. You have three minutes. Go!

"You have two minutes left. Here is a clue: the fifth word in the verse is 'Spirit.' Keep working.

"You have one minute to go. Here's another clue: the first five words are 'But when he, the Spirit.' "

Sharing Bible Learning

"The seniors have demonstrated their superiority—at least in unscrambling our verse today. They finished first, followed by the sophomores and then the juniors. Let's read the unscrambled verse aloud together.

"Our key verse reminds us that the Spirit of God is present with us to guide us into all truth. That is an important thought in our continuing study of the role of the Holy Spirit in the life of the believer. Let's turn to John 16 in our Bibles and give some further thought to this important concept."

SECRET MESSAGE PUZZLE

Purpose: That learners discover key words and/or phrases for a lesson by solving a jigsaw puzzle.

Materials
- ☐ A simple jigsaw puzzle with 30-40 pieces
- ☐ A felt marker
- ☐ Two sheets of sturdy poster board or cardboard

Procedure
1. Teacher assembles the jigsaw puzzle on a sheet of poster board. Then teacher turns the puzzle over by carefully laying poster board on top of the puzzle, lifting the puzzle from the table in between two sheets of poster board and turning it over.
2. Teacher writes a "secret message"—a key verse, statement or personal message from the teacher—on the back side of the completed puzzle, using a felt marker. Puzzle is then disassembled and returned to its container.
3. Learners assemble the puzzle in class, turn it over and read the "secret message."

Variations
1. Secret message puzzles may be used to communicate class announcements instead of verses or statements from the lesson.
2. A larger, more complex jigsaw puzzle may be used over a period of several weeks, with learners completing small sections each week. The "secret message" then might have relevance to the entire unit.
3. Pieces of the jigsaw puzzle may be mailed to learners prior to the class session with a note encouraging them to bring their puzzle pieces to help complete the puzzle. Any missing learners will mean missing pieces—illustrating the importance of class participation.

Example

Getting Started

Sample teacher instructions for using a secret message puzzle in an Approach activity:

"Welcome to class today! As others are still on their way, I would like to direct your attention to a jigsaw puzzle on the table. It is a very simple puzzle, and once you have completed it you may turn it over to discover a 'secret message' written on the back. Assemble it on the sheet of poster board you see there. Then to turn it over, place another sheet of poster board on top of the puzzle, carefully lift the puzzle while it is sandwiched between the poster boards, flip it over and return it to the table. You may start working together on the puzzle now. As others arrive, they will help you complete it."

Sharing Bible Learning

"You all worked together nicely to complete the puzzle, and you were successful in carefully turning the puzzle over to discover the 'secret message' on the back. Let's read the message aloud together.

"The secret message puzzle was an enjoyable way to get us started on our study for today—a discussion of God's shepherding qualities. Let's all turn to Psalm 23 and discover some ways God is like a shepherd."

Jr. High   Sr. High

ASSIGNED READING

Purpose: That learners explore resource material relevant to the lesson prior to the class session.

Materials
☐ Resource material for learners to read (books, magazines, articles, etc.)
☐ Copies of reading assignment for each learner

Procedure
1. Teacher determines specific reading assignments enough in advance to prepare written copies of the assignment for each learner.
2. Learners research elements of the lesson theme as directed by the reading assignment in preparation for class discussion.
3. During the class session, learners relate their discoveries from the reading assignment.

Variations
1. Different class members or groups may be given different reading assignments to provide a greater variety of research data for the classroom discussion.
2. Assigned reading may be restricted to Scripture passages relevant to the lesson (i.e. read from several different versions, read once each day during the week, etc.).
3. Assigned reading may follow the lesson with a brief feedback opportunity given during the next lesson.

Examples
The following reading assignments were distributed in preparation for a lesson from Romans 13:1-7 focusing on the responsibility of Christians to submit to governmental authorities. The assignments were given to different learners one week prior to the class session:

Assignment A: In preparation for our lesson next week, please read Romans 13:1-7 once each day and jot down any insights or questions you have regarding the theme of a Christian's relationship to governmental authorities.

Assignment B: In preparation for our lesson next week, please read Romans 13:1-7 this week in as many different versions of the New Testament as you can. As you read, jot down any insights or questions you have regarding the theme of a Christian's relationship to governmental authorities.

Assignment C: In preparation for our lesson next week, please read Romans 13:1-7 early in the week and summarize in one sentence Paul's instruction concerning our relationship to governmental authorities. Then during the rest of the week, read three or four different news magazines and jot down specific areas which apply to the Scripture and what a Christian's response should be.

Getting Started
Sample teaching instructions for using assigned reading in a Bible Exploration activity:

"Our lesson next week centers on such an interesting theme that it is deserving of a little advance preparation. The Scripture passage we will be studying talks about a Christian's responsibility to governing authorities—sometimes a very controversial issue! In order to get the best mileage from our discussion next week, I am distributing some reading assignments. Tenth graders will be receiving Assignment A, eleventh graders will get Assignment B and twelfth graders will get Assignment C. I want to encourage you to give attention to your assignment and come prepared next week for a great learning experience. By the way, to help you follow through on your assignment, I will have donuts and cocoa here for all who can report a completion of their task."

Sharing Bible Learning

"I want to thank you for your faithful involvement in our three reading assignments this week. I'm sure the stimulating research topic motivated you to get into the Scriptures and other resources in preparation for today's lesson. Or was it the donuts and cocoa?! Now let's share our response to the assignments. First, what about the sophomores? What insights or questions came to mind as you read Romans 13:1-7 during the week?"

RESEARCH ACTIVITIES

BOOK REPORT

Purpose: That learners investigate specific books relevant to the lesson or unit theme prior to the class or during the unit.

Materials
☐ Books for learners to borrow or buy
☐ Copies of book report assignment for involved learners

Procedure
1. Teacher determines specific books which will complement lesson or unit theme and prepares copies of the book report assignment for learners who will be involved.
2. Learners read the assigned books in the allotted time and complete book report assignment.
3. Learners share their book reports with the rest of the class.

Variations
1. Book report assignments may be given only to a limited number of class members (gifted or interested readers) while other members receive different research assignments.
2. Different learners or groups may read different books on the same theme.
3. Some books may be read in class by chapters or sections over an extended study of a theme. The teacher or appointed class members may read aloud for a portion of the class.
4. A library of books pertinent to the theme of class sessions, plus other good reading material, is a profitable addition to any classroom.

Example
   One class of learners was involved in a study of the life of Abraham, focusing on Abraham's example of faith. During the unit of study, several book reports were assigned which directed learners to read biographies of modern day men of faith whose experiences of trusting God paralleled those of Abraham. Books were assigned on the lives of George Mueller, Dwight L. Moody, C.T. Studd and other recognized pioneers of the faith. During each class session in the unit, one or more of the book reports were presented orally and class members discussed the comparisons between Abraham and the men of faith they had read about. The assignment brought the faith experiences of Abraham into focus through the contemporary faith experiences of biographed individuals.

Getting Started
   Sample teacher instructions for using book reports in a Bible Exploration activity:
   "As we launch into a several-week study of the life of Abraham, we will be looking especially at the faith expressed in this man chosen by God to be the father of the Hebrews. As we look at this man of faith in the Old Testament, it will be helpful for us to look at some other people who are closer to our time and see how faith looks in a contemporary setting. In order to help us get a good look at some

contemporary people of faith, I have selected several biographies of people who have lived in the twentieth century and exhibited the same life of faith as Abraham did. I would like to invite several of you to volunteer to read one of these books and then report back to us briefly during our study of Abraham during the next several weeks what you have learned about faith from your reading. Who would like to read the biography of George Mueller, a giant of faith?"

Sharing Bible Learning

"We have looked at how Abraham responded to situations where there was no alternative but to trust God. George Mueller was faced with several situations like that. Cindee recently read the biography of George Mueller and is now going to tell us what she learned about faith from this man's life."

RESEARCH ACTIVITIES

CENSUS/SURVEY

Purpose: That learners gather facts, information and/or opinions relating to a lesson or unit theme from a large sampling of people. NOTE: A census records *facts* and a survey records *opinions*.

Materials
☐ Duplicated copies of the census/survey form
☐ Copies of instructions for completing forms
☐ Pens or pencils

Procedure
1. Learners work with the teacher in developing a census/survey form which will assist them in reaching the lesson or unit goals.
2. Learners administer the census/survey to a predetermined number of persons and tabulate the results.
3. Census/survey results are integrated into the lesson or unit study.

Variations
1. A census/survey may be taken within the church's community or neighborhood to determine local needs which the church may be able to meet.
2. A census/survey may be used as an outreach tool—inquiring about people's religious views and then distributing material or fostering discussion concerning Christianity.
3. Youth may administer a census/survey to parents, church adults, peers, community at large or any combination of individuals or groups.

Example
The census/survey on page 113 was conducted among the adults in the church by a group of youth studying the importance of personal prayer time in the life of the Christian, based on Matthew 6:5-15.

Getting Started
Sample teacher instructions for using census/survey in a Bible Exploration activity:

"Last week we identified several questions we would like to ask the adults in our church about the subject of personal, private prayer. Today we have discussed some of the principles for the Christian's personal prayer life as we found them in Matthew 6:5-15. In addition to the principles we have discovered, we have much yet to learn about the practice of personal prayer. One way to gain this information is by asking several Christians we know about their prayer experience. We have prepared a survey based on the questions we formulated last week which should help us in gaining some insight into the practical aspect of personal prayer. During the week to come, interview as many adults and teenagers in our church as you can, by asking them the questions on the form. Record their answers and we will share the results together in class next week. Take as many copies of the survey as you think you will use."

Sharing Bible Learning

"Did you find the administering of the survey to be as exciting and interesting as I did? I learned a lot from the people I talked to, didn't you? Now it's time to compare our findings. First, would you please arrange your collection of completed surveys into four stacks: Teenage males, adult males, teenage females and adult females.

"I'm going to arrange our class into four groups and ask each group to take one of the four stacks for tabulation. You might want to determine the average number of times the people in your category have personal prayer time each week; average time spent per prayer time, and compile their comments on the other questions. After a time of working together with the surveys, we will compare answers."

PERSONAL PRAYER SURVEY

NAME (optional) _____ AGE _____ SEX _____

How many years have you been a Christian? _____

How often during the week do you have a personal, private prayer time? _____

How much time do you spend in your prayer time? _____

What else do you do as part of your prayer time (read the Bible, meditate, etc.)?
_____

Do you have a pattern that you follow during your prayer time? _____
   If so, please describe briefly: _____

What do you find to be the most difficult thing about your personal prayer
   time?_____

What do you find to be the most rewarding thing about your personal prayer
   time?

_____

What improvements would you like to see in your personal prayer time? _____
_____

FIELD TRIP

Purpose: That learners experience an off-campus learning opportunity which will parallel and complement in-class studies.

Materials
☐ Duplicated copies of field trip information (destination, what to bring, mode of transportation, purpose of the trip, etc.) for learners and parents

Procedure
1. Teacher determines an off-campus destination which would serve the need of helping to accomplish lesson or unit goals.
2. Teacher makes preparations regarding time, transportation, materials needed, parents' permission, etc.
3. Learners participate in field trip, gleaning vital information and/or experience.
4. Learners discuss their off-campus experience in light of lesson or unit goals.

Variations
1. Teachers can take learners on simulated field trips to Bible locations (e.g. a hilly area when the "Sermon on the Mount" is reenacted, a room in the church decorated like the inside of the Tabernacle, etc.).
2. Field trips may be arranged during classtime, or an extended classtime, where learners complete their Bible study projects in a location suggested by the lesson aims.
3. Extended field trips may be planned in conjunction with, or addition to, retreats.

Examples
The following list itemizes several possible field trip opportunities:
- Visiting another church to observe and discuss different modes of worship
- Visiting a church of a different ethnic constituency, cultural or socio-economic stratum
- Arranging to have a lesson on Paul's imprisonment in a local vacant jail cell
- Traveling through a "skid row" area in preparation for discussing Jesus' comments concerning the poor
- Visiting a museum to view artifacts from a Bible period being studied
- Attending a special youth program or rally which parallels lesson themes
- Taking an extended trip to visit foreign or home missions stations

Getting Started
Sample teacher instructions for using a field trip in a Bible Exploration activity:

"Next week we will continue our study of the book of Acts in a unique way. Acts chapter 16 relates the experience of Paul and Silas in prison. And to help us get a real feel for what their experience might have been like, we will be taking a field trip to the city jail and having our class meet in a vacant cell. We will get to feel the bars and meet the jailers, who will lock us in during the time of the lesson. The sheet I am now distributing has all the information, including a slip for your parents to sign and return giving us permission to put you in jail! Note the time we must meet to leave and other details concerning what to bring. After we study Acts 16 together in the cell, we will discuss the experience together."

Sharing Bible Learning

"It has been quite an experience sitting in this cell during the past forty minutes, talking about Paul and Silas. I have a better idea how they might have been feeling about imprisonment. Imagine that you might have been locked up here in the city jail for sharing your faith at school. What would be some of the thoughts going through your mind? What would you be praying about?"

Jr. High   Sr. High

INDUCTIVE STUDY

Purpose: That learners become involved in a direct, methodical, in-depth study of the Bible, using resources available and focusing on life application. (Inductive Bible study leads learners to discover a specific Bible truth, make a general life application, and then focus on a specific way to apply that truth to his/her daily life.)

Materials
☐ Bible for each learner
☐ Bible study resource materials (Bible dictionary, concordance, commentaries, etc.)
☐ Duplicated copies of inductive Bible study questions (see "Examples" section).
☐ Pens and pencils

Procedure
1. Teacher provides a setting suitable for study (tables and writing supplies), Bible study materials and copies of inductive Bible study questions.
2. Individuals or groups working together use Bible study materials to answer the inductive Bible study questions.
3. Learners share their discoveries with each other through teacher-led discussion.

Variation
Inductive Bible study assignments can be individual out-of-class research assignments. An in-class resource book library can be a valuable asset to learners using the inductive method.

Examples
Inductive study involves the learners in studying the Bible in a methodical and practical way. It follows the basic format of:
1. What does the Bible say?
2. What does it mean?
3. What does it mean to me?

Often these three questions alone are enough to stimulate in-depth study.

However, the same format can be expanded to include more specific questions which will help the learners become more detailed in their study. The following set of Bible study questions are designed for an inductive study of James 1:1-8:
1. What ways does James instruct Christians to handle trials they encounter?
2. What results does James promise when a believer responds to trials correctly?
3. What happens when a person asks for wisdom but does not believe that God will provide it?
4. Why is it important for a person to rejoice in his trials?
5. What keeps Christians today from rejoicing in trials?
6. Why is it important to ask for wisdom in trials?
7. What keeps Christians today from asking for wisdom?
8. Why is it important to have faith when asking for wisdom?
9. What keeps Christians from believing that God supplies wisdom?

10. When have you experienced trials and made the right responses? What were the results?
11. In what area of your life are you presently facing trials?
12. What response do you need to make to your present trials?

Getting Started

Sample teacher instructions for using inductive study in a Bible Exploration activity.

"Sometimes it is helpful to us to really 'dig in' to God's Word and ask ourselves, 'What is God saying? What does it mean? What does it mean to me?' In fact, those three questions, as simple as they may be, can serve as an effective Bible study tool to open up our understanding to God's Word. As we look into the first eight verses of James 1 today, I invite you to use any resource materials on the front table you may need to help you answer these three questions as you see them written on the chalkboard. Work alone for 15 minutes answering the questions, then we will share what we have found with one another."

Sharing Bible Learning

"I appreciate the way in which you have given yourselves to some serious Bible study in the last quarter hour. And I think you have noticed how helpful some of the resource books can be in helping us get into God's Word. Let's take some time now to share with one another what we have discovered. Let's start with the first question, 'What does the Bible say?' Let's talk about the basic message of these verses as you perceived it. Who would like to comment first?"

Jr. High   Sr. High

RESEARCH AND REPORT

Purpose: That learners gain specific information on certain questions or problems through research.

Materials
☐ Duplicated copies of research question or problem
☐ Research resources (Bibles, Bible dictionary, Bible atlas, encyclopedia, etc.)
☐ Writing paper
☐ Pens and pencils

Procedure
1. Teacher provides a setting suitable for research (tables and writing supplies), resource materials and copies of research question(s) or problem(s).
2. Individuals or groups working together use resource materials to gain information on specific Bible study questions or problems.
3. Teacher guides learners in sharing their discoveries and summarizes the main points.

Variations
1. Research and report projects may be assigned for out-of-class work with learners reporting their findings in subsequent class sessions.
2. Research projects may be assigned to learners who ask important questions which are not pertinent to the lesson being studied (e.g., "That's a good question, Sybil, and we need to give that important consideration at some time in the near future. Would you do a little research on that outside of class and be ready to share what you find at the beginning of class next week?").

Example
The following list itemizes several sample topics which would serve as good research and report projects:
● Historical background for a biblical event or person
● Geographical setting (topography, weather, elevation, etc.) of biblical events
● Study of biblical weights and measures
● Cultural characteristics of the various peoples of the Bible
● In-depth studies of biblical characters
● Greek and Hebrew word studies

Getting Started
Sample teacher instructions for using research and report in a Bible Exploration activity:
"I am anticipating our Bible study in the book of Daniel and I know we will learn a great deal from God's Word that will help us in our everyday lives. But before we look into the book of Daniel itself, it will be helpful for us to know some of the information on key persons and places in the book. Today we are going to get involved in research projects which will help paint a background picture for our Bible study. Our three learning groups will focus on three different 'research and

report' projects. Notice on your worksheets that group one will be finding out all they can about Babylon, the region where Daniel and the rest of the Hebrews were in captivity. Group two will be researching King Nebuchadnezzar, the ruler of Babylon during the time of Daniel's captivity. Group three will be researching the Chaldeans, the astrologers who served Nebuchadnezzar in Babylon. The front table contains numbers of resource books—atlases, encyclopedia, dictionaries, commentaries—which you may investigate to gain as much information as you can on your subject. At the conclusion of our study time, group one will be reporting on Babylon with a 'travel agent's report' on the area. Group two will report on Nebuchadnezzar in the format of an 'FBI intelligence report.' And group three will describe the Chaldeans to us from the perspective of the king's employment office. Your projects are explained completely on your worksheet. I will be available to assist if I can."

Sharing Bible Learning

"You have discovered a wealth of information in these three key background areas. Let's report to each other so that we can all gain from the work each group has done. Group one represents the Mid-East Travel Service and will now report to us all the details they have found on Babylon."

Jr. High   Sr. High

DISPLAYS AND EXHIBITS

Purpose: That learners summarize their discoveries from a unit of Bible study by displaying their work in the classroom.

Materials
☐ All learner classwork from a unit of study (art, writing, etc.)
☐ Wall and/or table for display
☐ Display decorations and supplies (colored paper, tape, push pins, etc.)

Procedure
1. Teacher designates an area of the classroom for display before beginning a unit of study.
2. Teacher and class members decorate the area in preparation for displaying student work.
3. Each week, teacher and learners add completed classwork to room display.
4. At the conclusion of the unit, learners invite parents and friends to view the completed display.

Variations
1. Displays and exhibits may be placed in church foyer, library or other prominent location for the enjoyment of a greater number.
2. The final session of the unit may be used for display preparation and/or open house for parents, other classes, etc.

Example
The sketches on pages 121 and 122 illustrate a classroom display during the four-session unit of study on parables.

Getting Started
Sample teacher instructions for introducing a unit classroom display/exhibit:
"During the next four sessions we are going to be looking at some of the fascinating parables Jesus told in the Gospels. And to keep track of the exciting discoveries we make in the course of our Bible studies, we are going to use an area of the classroom for a display called 'Principles from Parables.' During each session, we will add to the display some of the work we do in class. At the end of the unit, we will host an open house so that your parents and other people can enjoy seeing your quality work. Together, let's make our display something we will be proud of."

Sharing Bible Learning
Sample teacher comments as the display is completed:
"I think we have done a beautiful job of showing our discoveries in this display. I also think your parents and friends will be impressed with the quality of your work. As you look at the display and think about the past four sessions, what was the most important thing you learned from the parables we discussed?"

Session 1

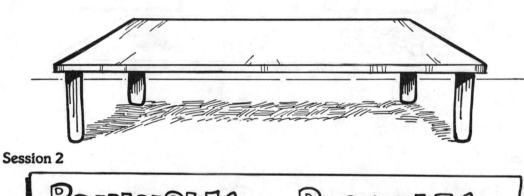

Session 2

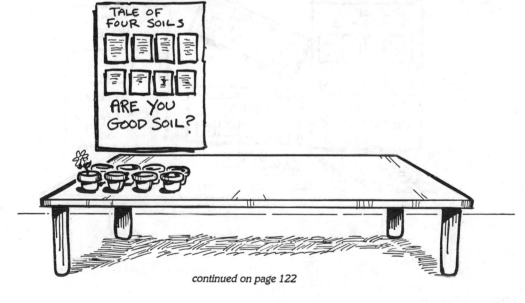

continued on page 122

Session 3

Session 4

122

MISCELLANEOUS ACTIVITIES

MODELS

Purpose: That learners visualize in three dimensions Bible objects, buildings and geographic locations in conjunction with discovering Bible truth.

Materials
☐ Supplies needed for model to be created
☐ Written instructions for model construction

Procedure
1. Teacher gathers supplies and prepares written instructions for model construction.
2. Learners follow instructions and construct models in conjunction with Bible study.
3. Learners display models and discuss scriptural principles related to their creations.

Variations
1. Many models may need two or more class periods for completion. Model construction may be planned as a unit long (2-3 weeks or more) activity.
2. Bible costumes, either life-size or miniature, provide a creative challenge in the model category.
3. Many models may be placed on long-term display somewhere in the church after the unit of study is completed.

Examples
The following sketch illustrates a model of the crucifixion scene, showing many of the implements which were present on the premises during the biblical narrative in Matthew 27:32-54.

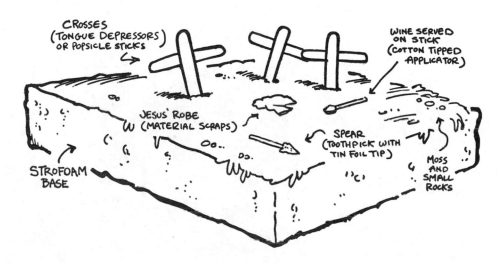

CROSSES
(TONGUE DEPRESSORS)
OR POPSICLE STICKS

WINE SERVED
ON STICK
(COTTON TIPPED
APPLICATOR)

JESUS' ROBE
(MATERIAL SCRAPS)

SPEAR
(TOOTHPICK WITH
TIN FOIL TIP)

MOSS
AND
SMALL
ROCKS

STROFOAM
BASE

Additional possibilities for models are:

OBJECTS	BUILDINGS
Tools	Tabernacle
Weapons	Temple
Household articles	Houses

LOCATIONS	COSTUMES
Jerusalem	Priest
Jericho (in Joshua's time)	Roman centurion
Bethlehem and the hills	John the Baptist

Getting Started

Sample teacher instructions for using a model in a Bible Exploration activity:

"During the next three weeks we are studying the crucifixion of our Lord Jesus Christ as recorded in Matthew 26 and 27. In order to help us visualize more clearly the crucifixion and some of the accompanying events, we are going to put together a model of the scene using simple, everyday objects. Part of our lesson time each week will be used to add to our model. Today we will begin by preparing a styrofoam block to serve as the base which will hold the three crosses. But first, let's turn to Matthew 26:47 and look at the first events which led to the cross."

Sharing Bible Learning

"As we put this model together over the next few weeks, it will be good for us to remember that everything we construct for this miniature scene of Golgotha was part of a purpose which included you and me. The objects of the crucifixion were all part of God's love plan for our salvation. As we work on the styrofoam base today, let's talk about some of the specific things we are thankful for in the suffering our Lord endured. For example, I am thankful that Jesus was committed to obey the Father's will even though it caused him great pain and ended in His death. What are you most thankful for?"

MISCELLANEOUS ACTIVITIES

QUIZZES AND TESTS

Purpose: That learners review and summarize their discoveries over a lesson, unit or quarter.

Materials
☐ A copy of the quiz for each learner (photocopied or mimeographed)
☐ Pens or pencils

Procedure
1. At the conclusion of a predetermined course of study (lesson unit or quarter), teacher gives each learner a copy of the quiz designed to help him/her review the material.
2. Learners work alone or in groups to complete the quiz in the required amount of time.
3. Teacher reviews correct answers of the quiz with learners to reinforce discoveries.

Variations
1. Quizzes can be arranged in a number of formats—question and answer, multiple choice, true-false, matching, essay, etc.
2. Quizzes may be written on poster paper or overhead transparencies for classroom display (learners write answers on blank sheets of paper).
3. Quizzes may be conducted in a light vein—using humor in the questions, offering simple prizes or awards for success, etc.
4. Brief quizzes may precede each lesson, reviewing the main ideas of the previous lesson's study.

Examples
The following quiz was designed to help learners review the highlights of a study of Daniel 3—the image of gold and the fiery furnace. The quiz models several formats and utilizes humor.
1. The man who made the image of gold was King
   a. Tut.
   b. Kong.
   c. Nebuchadnezzar.
   d. Darius.
2. The image which the king made was _____ feet high.
3. True or False: According to Daniel 3:4, whenever a person saw the golden image, he was to bow down and worship.
4. Verse 6 states that whoever does not fall down and worship the image will be
   a. thrown into a blazing furnace.
   b. thrown into the lion's den.
   c. detained after class.
   d. sent to the principal.
5. Three Jews who did not serve the king's gods or worship the image he made were S_____, M_____ and A_____.

6. True or False: The king was so angry at the three Jews' refusal to worship the image that he heated the furnace seven times hotter than usual.
7. According to verse 25, the king looked into the furnace and saw
   a. charcoal briquets.
   b. four men walking around in the fire.
   c. three men walking around in the fire.
   d. fire.
8. After the Jews were removed from the furnace, the king said: "Praise be to God who has sent his _____ and rescued his servants."

Getting Started

Sample teacher instructions for using a quiz in a Bible Exploration activity:

"Last week we enjoyed studying together from the third chapter of Daniel—an exciting true story of the courage of three young men in the face of an attempt on their lives. Before we move into chapter 4, let's review the highlights of what we discussed last week. In order to do that, I'm passing out a brief quiz on our lesson last week. Don't worry! This quiz is designed to help us review our study of God's Word—not to give you a grade. Work quietly and individually for 3-4 minutes completing your copy of the quiz. Then we will review the correct answers together."

Sharing Bible Learning

"I can see that you enjoyed the quiz and that most of you have completed it. Let's use the next few minutes to review our answers. Question 1: 'The man who made the image of gold was King. . . .' Not King Tut or King Kong, but King Nebuchadnezzar. What are some other things we have learned about King Nebuchadnezzar?"

SERVICE PROJECTS

Purpose: That learners practice application of specific Bible principles through practical projects and activities.

Materials
☐ Supplies needed for specific project to be undertaken.

Procedure
1. Learners study Bible principles related to caring and serving, with a focus on the practical elements of applying those principles.
2. Teacher and learners together design and plan practical expressions of service which will reflect the principles studied. Planning may take place during class time.
3. Class members carry through with their service project and evaluate success based on principles in focus.

Variations
1. Class members may request that church leadership bodies suggest service projects which would fulfill application of Bible study principles.
2. Service projects are perfect opportunities to involve parents in activities with youth.

Examples
The following suggestions are a sample of possible service projects to involve youth in practical application of Bible principles:
- Visit nursing homes and/or homebound church members.
- Provide Saturday or Sunday meal service to homebound church members.
- Clean up the community through neighborhood trash pickup service.
- Volunteer to teach Bible school for a smaller, understaffed church.
- Offer free babysitting for young mothers' evening clubs.
- Provide free janitorial service for the church one week.
- Offer to provide a continuing service to the church (prepare floral displays, weed flower beds, serve as ushers for one of the weekly services, etc.).
- Volunteer as big brothers/sisters for church or community children in single parent homes.
- Sponsor a fund-raising event to purchase needed supplies for the church (hymnals, nursery toys, outdoor plants, etc.).

Getting Started
Sample teacher instructions for using a service project in a Bible Exploration activity:

"We have been studying scriptural principles for serving those who are less fortunate than ourselves, as suggested by Paul's brief instruction in 1 Thessalonians 5:15: 'Help the weak.' We have now come to the place where we need to practice what we have been learning by giving ourselves a specific project which will help us carry through with the Lord's instruction to us. If we were determined to obey Paul's command in 1 Thessalonians 5:14 to 'help the weak,' we would first need to identify who the 'weak' are, and then how we might help them. Let's brainstorm on the first question—who are the 'weak' who may need our help? Yes, Laurie, some of the aged are weak. Thank you, Carl, I agree that there are mentally retarded in the community who are weak and need help. (Continue brainstorming.)

"We have brainstormed a list of the 'weak' who need our help. And we have decided that we want to help some of the older church members in some way. Let's now discuss some ways we could help the senior citizens here at the church. Yes, Serina, visit them at home. Yes, Marci, bringing a hot meal to them regularly— especially those who cannot cook for themselves. (Continue listing ideas; then have group choose one.)

"It's decided then that we will volunteer to cook and deliver a hot meal each Saturday for one month to the four ladies who are unable to cook for themselves."

Sharing Bible Learning

"We have completed our commitment to 'help the weak' by preparing and delivering meals to four shut-ins. Let's talk about what we have done. What has impressed you most about our project? Thank you for that insight, Ben. I agree that some of the 'romance' of the project wore off and it became 'work' which took some of our valuable time on Saturday. We were left with the discipline of carrying through with our commitment even when we didn't *feel* like serving. And isn't that just what Jesus did in serving us—going to the cross even when He might have preferred another way?"

128